A ROYAL
PRIESTHOOD
ARISING

You are worthy to take the scroll and to open its seals, because you were slain, and with your blood you purchased men for God from every tribe and language and people and nation. You have made them to be a kingdom and priests to serve our God, and they will reign.

REVELATION 5:9–10

As the kingdoms of this world shake and crumble, the kingdom of our God emerges brighter and brighter, *strong, unshakeable.*

A kingdom and priests to serve our God, *a royal priesthood arising...*

(All scripture taken from NIV, unless otherwise noted)

© 2018 Deborah Goodwater
ISBN-13: 978-0-692-08745-9
Printed in the USA

Cover design by James Nesbit
Inside design by Lorinda Gray/Ragamuffin Creative

A ROYAL PRIESTHOOD

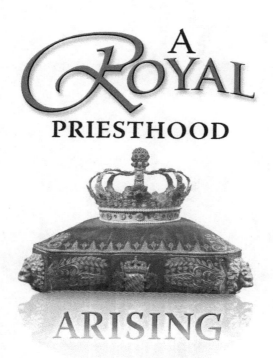

ARISING

DEBORAH GOODWATER

Introduction

God is issuing a fresh call for His church to rise up as His royal priesthood in the earth. He desires that we embrace this call and the preparation of His Spirit to operate in this calling. He desires that all His children walk with Him in this, for this is not something for just a few "superspiritual" people but for anyone with a hungry heart to know Christ, no matter who you are, where you have come from, or what you have done in your past.

Where the Old Testament reality of the priests was a foreshadowing of what Christ would fulfill, the New Testament reality of a priest is fully grounded in what Christ has fulfilled, so its basis is love, having our hearts grounded in the heights, widths, and depths of His love. All have access to His love, every tribe and language and people and nation, transformed by His love into a kingdom and priests.

In 2009, the Lord spoke into my heart His idea for me to write this book one day when I was sitting with Him. It was not something I had previously considered or desired. My heart was awakened with expectancy that He had sown things in my heart that He wanted to have written down. Many years since that time of continuing to sit at His feet in the secret place and then walk out what He was saying, here is the fruit of a seed sown in my heart that day. As He spoke to me, my heart was stirred with faith that He wanted to awaken hearts to rise up as priests of the Lord. I began to desire to walk deeper into His heart and see the revelation He wanted to share that would bring honor and praise to the only one who is worthy, our soon-coming King and Bridegroom, and the High Priest of our faith, Jesus Christ.

As God began to show me there were things He desired to speak concerning His priesthood, I set my heart to receive increased spiritual understanding. The book of Daniel speaks of words being closed up and sealed until an appointed time (Daniel 12:9). Paul in the book of Colossians penned that his purpose in writing was for them to be encouraged in their hearts and united in love so they may have "the *full riches of complete understanding,* in order that they may know the mystery of God, namely, Christ, in whom are hidden ***all the treasures of wisdom and knowledge***" (Colossians 2:2). I believe there is an unveiling of God's timeless word, the Bible, so we are encouraged in our hearts with an ever-deepening vision of Christ that will prepare us as His priesthood to live in this next season of time.

As you read this book, I pray that your heart would be awakened with a fresh revelation of Christ, His love for you, and your calling in Him, and that you would be equipped by His Spirit to walk out that calling. I pray also that grace would be released on your heart to push past every limitation to lay hold of His great and glorious promises. Revelation 5:9 says that a new song is being sung around the throne:

> You are worthy to take the scroll and to open its
> seals because you were slain, and with your blood
> you purchased men for God from every tribe and

language and people and nation. You have made
them to be a kingdom and priests to serve our God,
and they will reign on the earth.

In this verse, the revelation is opened up to hearts that from Christ's finished work on the cross, He has purchased people from all nations to be a part of His kingdom. He desires that the realness of His kingdom would be opened up to hearts like tapping into a well.

The second part of this verse reveals that we are priests. God is issuing a call to come into a deeper experience as priests of the Lord ministering to Him and with Him. God's heart is revealed as we pursue understanding in this area that will equip His people for the glorious days in which we have the privilege of living.

While I was reading an old book a number of years back, I began to see some things in a new light. The words from David Wilkerson's book *Set the Trumpet to Thy Mouth* pierced my heart like hot coals in a new way, releasing a fresh burden and giving understanding to some words the Lord spoke to my heart as He began to prepare me to write this book. The Lord's words to me were, "The priests are being readied in the secret place with revelation for the times." As I read Rev. Wilkerson's book, the picture was painted in a fresh way of the darkness that is coming. This book releases not fear, but God's truth and ways. These words written over thirty years ago, from a man who has gone on to eternal glory, trumpet the call to prepare. The Lord is preparing His bride and teaching her to overcome in all situations. He is raising up a priesthood who will be fully devoted to Him. As we seek Him in the secret place, there is an unlocking of our hearts to release the glory of God from within. It is truly the hour for Christ to be revealed in His people. Therefore, "Arise, shine, for your light has come, and the glory of the Lord rises upon you. See, darkness covers the earth and thick darkness is over the peoples, but the Lord rises upon you and his glory appears over you" (Isaiah 60:1).

These verses speak of His glory that will arise during a time of great darkness. As His word is released, let our hearts be prepared to arise and shine in His light in this growing darkness. May Jesus Christ receive the reward of His suffering as a royal priesthood arises in the earth from every tongue and tribe and nation.

The sweet aroma of your word, Lord, touching
our hearts and awakening passion for You,
our soon coming King and Bridegroom.

Jesus, would you give to us revelation that will bring understanding of Your ways and your words. Our hearts are crying out to walk in the fullness of Your truth.

Holy Spirit, lead us into all truth.

Contents

1

Who Are the Priests?

In his first epistle, Peter declares a God-ordained calling intended to awaken the hearts of believers: "*You* are a chosen people, a royal priesthood, a holy nation, a people belonging to God, that you may declare the praises of Him who called you out of darkness into His wonderful light."

...a royal priesthood, a holy nation, a people belonging to God...

What comes to your mind when you think of a priest? Is it the Old Testament picture of a single man with flowing garments or the person ministering the word from a big lectern at the front of a church in liturgical garments? Have you ever considered that *you* are called to be a part of this royal priesthood and holy nation? Does your heart cry out to walk in all that Christ has for your life?

To move toward this truth being awakened in your life, you have to see it as a possibility. Do you desire to have your heart awakened to a greater reality of His love and His life moving in your heart? To begin this priestly ministry, do you realize you won't have to rush off to seminary or change anything in your life other than to position your heart in openness to Him so He can begin to join your heart to His heart?

I recall the time in my life as a young adult in college where I thought being close to Him would require certain roles in ministry. I can remember the ache of rejection I felt in my heart, the separation from Him that I experienced because of these false belief systems. Somehow, along the way, I had developed a way of thinking that the priests were those in full-time pastoral ministry and were the closest to God. It caused a pursuit in my heart to be in ministry. Through college, I had a very busy church ministry life, which I thought equated with knowing God. This pursuit to find God through ministering left me empty. Ministering for God in an effort to get to Him did nothing to appease the deep longings that filled my heart. In time, God in His love and mercy began to break in with His truth.

Out of college, I had been transferred to Omaha, Nebraska, with my job as a workers' compensation auditor. For several years prior to moving to Omaha, I had a growing hunger to learn to pray and go deeper in my relationship with Jesus. As I moved to a new city, I had an expectancy for new things of God.

As I settled into my new life, I began to seek God for His plan for this new season. I assumed this would mean launching into new ministry in this new place. He set me in a local community of believers, and as I asked the Lord to show me what He wanted me to do there at church, He spoke to me and said that He hadn't brought me to this new place to pick up and keep doing all my ministry activity. He said He had brought me to Omaha to teach me how to sit at His feet.

These words brought a quaking deep inside of me. God spoke loudly to my heart the verse out of 1 Samuel 15:22, "to obey is better than sacrifice." I knew His voice enough that I knew it was the Lord who was leading me in this. I set out to obey His word. I felt so unspiritual because I wasn't busy doing what I viewed was ministry for Him. As the ministry work was stripped away, the truth that much of my doing had its motivation rooted in a need to try to earn His love was soon revealed. My heart was shaken because without this work to bring Him, I was left unsure of His love and devotion for me. A giant fear rose up in my heart that was undetected to this point: Did God love me? It exposed that I was trying to earn His love through my works, but I didn't yet understand that He was leading me into the revelation that I still needed to learn: that apart from Jesus, I could not draw near and that my works could not earn His love. His love was freely given. As I began to come to Him, just to be with Him and have my heart opened to His work, I began to experience His holy presence in my heart. I began to see myself before Him and began to see that self is what separated me from Him. In those times of encounter with His living presence, pride and self-righteousness just fell away, and the knowledge deep in my heart that I could not bring Him anything in myself that would make Him love me was sown deeply in my heart. My heart was filled with the revelation of His love apart from anything I was doing for Him. His love began to heal my heart. I began to resist my mind-sets that tormented me that He did not love me because I was not busy for Him. I began to resist the expectations others had of me of what I should be doing for God. Roots of rejection began to be healed. Depression that I had battled through high school left. Fear of so many things began to go as His love washed over my heart. I began to experience strength in my heart that was not my own, but it came from the Holy Spirit in me, that caused me to continue to just listen to Him and obey His word to just come and be with Him. As my heart was released from these bondages of works, I could rest at His feet. I could drink deeply of His love apart from my own labors. I could spend time with Him with no other motivation but to know Him.

The Holy Spirit began to move on my heart with His living presence in a fresh way, drawing me by the love of God being revealed in my heart in a tangible way, meaning I could feel His love. As He moved in my heart, there was a washing with the word, healing wounds that had come throughout my life. The blood of Jesus was applied to my heart, which really does restore every broken place.

As I drew near to God in a new freedom to come just spend time with Him, the Holy Spirit began to awaken my heart in a new way to God's love for me. Out of this love, I began to have my heart moved in new ways with concern for people and situations where I would not normally be concerned. The study of the Bible was fresh and living. The Holy Spirit stirred my heart to apply in prayer different Scriptures He would put on my heart. After my mother's death a few years ago, I was looking through my mother's belongings. I found a sticky note in her Bible from years ago. She wrote that I had called her to tell her God was "breaking my heart for people in places I had never been." In that season in my early years in Omaha, my heart was beginning to come alive in His love for me and for others. I was being joined to Him in the freedom of His love, which was birthing a priestly calling.

Sitting with Christ in the Secret Place

When I read the account of God calling out the nation of Israel to Himself in Exodus 19:4, I see God's heart revealed to draw people close to Himself: "You yourselves have seen what I did to Egypt, and how I carried you on eagles' wings and brought you to Myself." God has carried us on eagles' wings to Himself through His Son, Jesus Christ. We have been set apart to love Him wholeheartedly. The righteous requirements of God's holiness preventing sinful man from coming close have been fully satisfied through Christ. Jesus has removed the barriers that separated us from God.

These next verses in Exodus 19 will trip us up and set us on performing to be close to God if we do not read these verses through the eyes of the new covenant of Jesus Christ.

"Now if you obey Me fully and keep my covenant, then out of all nations you will be My treasured possession. Although the whole earth is Mine, you will be for Me a kingdom of priests and a holy nation. These are the words you are to speak to the Israelites." And they all responded, "We will do everything the Lord has said."

How do we do this—obey Him fully and keep His covenant? God has given us a new covenant through the blood of His Son, Jesus Christ. It is a covenant of love, and to obey it fully, we must receive all that Christ did for us and come to rest in that work. We begin to sit at His feet. Jesus's words to us in John 15 call us to remain in His love. He wants to bring our hearts fully at rest in His love. His law of love is written on our hearts (Hebrews 8:10). Hearts of stone become hearts of flesh (Ezekiel 36:26). All know Him, from the least of them to the greatest (Hebrews 8:11).

The verses in the next chapter of Exodus are perhaps some of the saddest verses in scripture to me and reveal the human heart after the initial response of agreement to do all that the Lord would say: In Exodus 20:18, it states

> When the people saw the thunder and lightning and heard the trumpet and saw the mountain in smoke, they trembled with fear. They stayed at a distance and said to Moses, "Speak to us yourself and we will listen. But do not have God speak to us or we will die."

God was calling out a people to himself, to be His chosen people. When they saw the smoke and heard the lightning, they drew back in fear, stayed at a distance, and decided they wanted someone else speaking to them for God.

Revelation 1:12–14 is the revelation of Jesus standing in the middle of the lampstands. Jesus is revealed and is speaking to His church. In these verses, His eyes are described as like blazing fire. We will look more closely at His fire in later chapters. For now, I will just say it is the fire of His love and His purity. He desires to fill every heart with holy love that casts out all fear. His eyes of fire beckon us to His goodness, and they beckon us to draw close to Him in the secret place. God longs for His children to come close so He can speak personally to hearts. All have full access into His presence. The question is, will we draw near or stay at a distance when we begin to encounter the fire of His presence?

As the truth is awakened in our hearts that God wants us to come close and have relationship with Him, where can we go to meet with God? The children of Israel were called to go to a mountain where God came down in a cloud. Where is the place where God reveals Himself and speaks directly to us?

God is drawing us to come to meet with Him in the secret place of our hearts.

The Webster's dictionary definition of the word *secret* is "concealed from sight." Ask the Holy Spirit to establish the secret place in your life, the hidden life in Christ. This work of God is done in the secret place of your heart and is concealed from human sight. Meeting with Christ doesn't have to be reduced to only the times you are sitting before Him in a prayer room or by coming to a church service; it is our hearts before God in constant interaction. It is no longer about going to a certain place to meet with God. As we take time to draw away from our busy schedules just to sit with Him, our minds and hearts are set on things above. It becomes about drawing into God in the midst of our ordinary daily lives, learning to hear His voice above the roar of all the other voices as we train our hearts to rest in His presence. This is a lifelong adventure. We will need the constant companionship of the Holy Spirit on this journey. We have Jesus's words in John 14:16 to encourage us in this relationship with the Holy Spirit:

> And I will ask the Father, and he will give you another counselor, to be with you forever—the Spirit of truth. The world cannot accept him, because it neither sees him nor knows him. But you know him, for he lives with you and will be in you.

Jesus's promise remains today. He is not just with us; the Holy Spirit is in us. God gave us the Holy Spirit so we can be close to God—closer than we ever imagined. The Holy Spirit comes to be present with you to draw you into the secret place of your heart and bring you fully alive in Christ.

As we begin to interact with God in the secret place of our hearts, Christ becomes "alive" to us in our hearts by the power of Holy Spirit, shaking off all deadness of heart, and the "living word" is allowed to search to uncover and awaken hearts from a "reputation of being alive, but are dead" (Revelation 3:1). Prayer is about a relationship with God. Our prayer life will come alive as our hearts come alive to His presence living in our hearts. His word, the Bible, will come alive to us when He is free to move in our hearts. He touches our hearts with His living word, and suddenly we are alive again, awakened to what really matters: Jesus, the Word made flesh, making the word flesh in our lives. This means the Bible is no longer words on a page that we know in our heads, but it is being lived out from our hearts.

John's vision of Jesus in the book of Revelation describes Jesus with stars in his right hand, and a sharp two-edged sword comes out of His mouth. His face is like the sun in all its brilliance. As we sit with Christ in the secret place, His eyes of fire are gazing on us. May His word, which Hebrews 4:12 says is "a sword," penetrate us, "even to divide between soul and spirit." May our souls, consisting of the mind, will, and emotions, be set free from their power in our lives through His active word landing on our hearts. A yielding to His love that is higher and deeper and stronger than any other pursuit or drive begins to happen. Jesus is established as Lord over our mind, will, and emotions. May our spirits be awakened, coming alive as the atmosphere of our hearts are filled with His word, and finally, may our spirits be released by the Living Word into our high calling as sons and daughters who live as priests of the Lord, in the ordinary, everyday things of life. As you move through the pages of this book, let your heart be opened to the Holy Spirit's voice of what that looks like for you personally.

Sitting with Christ in Heaven's Realms

From this position of sitting with Christ in the secret place of our hearts comes an opening up of a greater reality. In the book of Revelation, the disciple John is on the island of Patmos. He had an invitation to come up into the spiritual realm, where he saw the throne of heaven.

> And the voice I had first heard speaking to me like a trumpet said, "come up here, and I will show you what must take place after this." At once I was in the Spirit, and there before me was a throne in heaven with someone sitting on it. (Revelation 4:1–2)

"Come up here in the Spirit." His natural circumstances remained the same, alone, imprisoned on a four- by eight-mile island. A spiritual reality was opened up that was not hindered by where he was. We begin to see that this priestly calling in Christ that we are being invited into cannot be contained or limited by our natural circumstances. This means it doesn't matter who you are, where you live, or what your occupation is. God is calling you to live in a spiritual reality above all of these natural realities. This priestly calling is a spiritual calling.

As priests of the Lord, we are called to live higher. There is a call of the Spirit to anyone who will hear to come up higher in the Spirit to what is happening around the throne of God. Our natural circumstances cannot restrict this open door. As we see Him by the word and by the Spirit, our hearts are being firmly set in the unshakeable truth that Jesus is the center of all things, and worship to Him is central in our lives.

> Day and night they never stop saying: Holy, holy, holy is the Lord God Almighty, who was, and is, and is to come. Whenever the living creatures give glory, honor and thanks to him who sits on the throne and who lives for ever and ever, the twenty-four elders fall down before him who sits on the throne, and worship him who lives for ever and ever. (Revelation 4:9)

The spiritual realm was opened up to John to see the activity of the throne room where Jesus is the center. He is seated on His throne. The apostle Paul in the book of Ephesians describes the way that has been opened up through Christ to bring all up higher in the Spirit.

> But because of his great love for us, God, who is rich in mercy, made us alive with Christ even when we were dead in transgressions—it is by grace you have been saved. And God raised us up with Christ and seated us with him. (Ephesians 2:4-6)

Our hearts are being moved into a position of sitting with Christ. We are raised up with Christ and seated with Him in the heavenly realm. This simply means that heaven's reality is becoming a greater reality than this present world. The Lord is establishing the truth of this reality deeply in our hearts. We learn to sit before Him, and our anxious minds and hearts come to stillness and rest as we see Him, high and lifted up over every situation. Our hearts being recalibrated into a place of all things in our lives bowing to His lordship. Our hearts are being trained to draw into His presence that abides in us. God's perspective for people and situations begin to invade our hearts, and we grow into a place of praying without ceasing. Day and night, there is continual worship in our hearts to King Jesus, with His will being declared on earth as it is in heaven. This does not mean we will have to move to a monastery to soak in silence.

A kingdom of priests is arising from every tribe and every language and people and nation. It is Christ's living body in the earth, joined to Him. *All* have a calling in Christ to be priests of the Lord. As we see His word, we see the door of possibility that has been opened up to His whole body rising up, ministering to Him in the secret place of our hearts, and living from this hidden place in Christ to release His power and presence to the world, every day, all through the day.

It is time for His church to rise up in a new way as His priests. Christ has made us to be priests to serve our God. Jesus Christ, our great High Priest, is the curtain by which we come in to have unbroken communion with God. Pass through this way and rise up in the sanctuary of His presence.

Here's a prayer:

> Jesus, reveal Your beauty and the glory of Your kingdom to us. May you be more real than anything we know of this present world. May our hearts be forever captured by Your love.

2

Jesus, a New and Living Way

Therefore, holy brothers, who share in the heavenly
calling, fix your thoughts on Jesus, the apostle and
high priest whom we confess.

Hebrews 3:1

In this chapter, as we look through the book of Hebrews, invite the
Holy Spirit to awaken your heart to a deeper revelation of the
beauty of Christ's work that frees our hearts from the old covenant with its rules and regulations that provided only temporary,
occasional access to God and opens up the new and living way that
gives us restored fellowship to God. Through restored daily fellowship
with God, our hearts get set free. There is true freedom that is available in Christ to the heart that this world knows nothing of. Let us no
longer settle to give mental assent to truths in the Bible that are not
being lived out. Let us draw near to God until true freedom is experienced—freedom from every form of fear and anxiety.

Hebrews 2:14 declares that through Christ's death, He destroyed
Satan's power and set us free from the fear of death. The power of all

death is broken. Jesus came to bring life. As we lose our old lives to follow Him, no matter how good or bad those old lives were, we find true life and freedom in Christ. We don't have to fear death in any form. Our hearts get set free from self-preservation, which simply means the protection of oneself from harm or death. It is a basic instinct in humans. Invite the Holy Spirit to reveal and remove any self-preservation operating in your life. We can trust God's way. It is good and leads to fullness of life. We don't have to fear death to self through embracing the cross of Christ any longer. The power of all death has been broken.

> Anyone who does not take his cross and follow me is not worthy of me. Whoever finds his life (holding on to our own life) will lose it, and whoever loses his life for my sake will find it. (Matthew 10:38)

Live Free

My father had his first encounter with the love of Christ that brings salvation when he was a young man. His life had been marked by a hard, abusive father in his formative years. After receiving Christ for salvation, he went off to Bible school to pursue God's call. My mother's journals tell the story that his past life still plagued him, and those years were filled with rage and depression in his heart that would affect their home life. He would graduate from Bible school, get ordained in the denomination he was a part of, and begin to pastor a church.

Through high school, my memories involved going to church with him as the pastor and our home life being filled with the cloud of anger and depression that would begin to consume my own heart with depression and a cloud of hopelessness that left me feeling like I wanted to die. The only thing that prevented me from entertaining thoughts of taking my own life for very long was the fear of eternal separation from Jesus, who I knew to be real, but He seemed so far away.

As God led my heart into freedom in Christ that I shared about in the first chapter, my heart was also moved toward a different perspective of my dad in my adult years. Forgiveness toward him came to my heart, and a longing to see him know the same freedom that can only be found in Christ that my own heart had found.

Many years would pass, and I would find myself still praying for his freedom. He talked often of wanting to die so he could go to heaven. He seemed to have no hope that there was freedom in this life from the bondages that weighed his heart down. He was diagnosed with cancer, and the day I got the call that his kidneys were shutting down, I made arrangements to fly back from Alaska to see him. I flew through the night, not knowing if he would still be alive when I got to Kansas City. When I walked into the hospital room, my family was gathered around his bed. Though still alive, he was not really coherent. The Lord would speak to my heart when I got to his room that I wasn't to leave till he passed. As the day went by, he seemed to be hanging on for no apparent reason. In the evening, different ones would leave to go home. At about 11:30 p.m., the only ones left were my mom, who had gone to lay down in a bed in the room, and my niece and me. I felt prompted by the Holy Spirit to read over him Romans 8. As I got to the part that said "the creation itself will be liberated from its bondage to decay and brought into the glorious freedom of the children of God," it became more of God's declaration to him as he prepared to pass from this life. The Holy Spirit led me to declare to him, "Dad, go be free in Christ." Within a short time, his eyes would flutter, and he would take his last breaths, and he would go home to be with Jesus, free at last. The glory of God filled my own heart in a new way at his passing, and I carried a deep sense of God's weighty presence that I could strongly feel for several days in my heart. I also sensed a fresh expectancy for a freedom in Christ that is available to all.

About six months later, my mom would have a vision of my dad. He was standing on the sea of glass that is described in the book of Revelation, his arms raised high in worship, the veils of this life gone, His heart was totally free in Christ's presence.

> The former regulation is set aside because it was weak and useless (for the law made nothing perfect), and a better hope is introduced by which we draw near to God. (Hebrews 7:18–19)

Hebrews 10 states that "the law is only a shadow of the good things that are coming-not the realities themselves." Following rules will not bring His life to our hearts.

> For this reason it (the law) can never, by the same sacrifices repeated endlessly year after year, make perfect those who draw near in worship... But those sacrifices are an annual reminder of sins, because it is impossible for the blood of bulls and goats to take away sins.

We are dead to sin because of Christ's sacrifice, alive to Christ and all that He has done for us. Our hearts day by day are being renewed and strengthened in this perfect sacrifice of His love. Because of His sacrifice, there is no more need to bring sacrifices to get to God. As our hearts are strengthened in His love, we stop offering Him things He isn't asking for. From out of the new covenant that has a permanent priesthood, our hearts are set free to simply be worshipers of God.

This is our calling, to live free in Christ (Galatians 5:1). We are free to be hidden in Christ, unconstrained from pursuits and running to other things, even ministry, or even focusing on what others are called to do that would blind us to our true calling, that of pure, simple devotion to Christ. It is the hidden place, secure in Him, free in His love. His words to Martha in Luke echo in our own spirits and set our hearts free just to sit and be with Him. "Martha, only one thing is needed." This is true freedom—having our souls fully satisfied *in* Him and by Him. We are saved completely in His love, unshaken by our circumstances. The power of the cross actively at work in our lives, receiving wine and milk that this world knows not of, not able to buy with this world's currencies (money systems), not dependent on this world's economies.

Isaiah 55:1 declares a promise,

> Come, all you who are thirsty, come to the waters; and you who have no money, come, buy, and eat! Come, buy wine and milk without money and without cost. Why spend money on what is not bread, and your labor on what does not satisfy?

For us to live free in Christ, we must be weaned from other sources of dependency that our hearts look to and the world looks to, to save us. There is new wine and living water freely given to those who come to Him. He has promised that His love and His peace are unshakeable and always available. "Though the mountains be shaken and the hills be removed, yet my unfailing love for you will not be shaken nor my covenant of peace be removed, says the Lord" (Isaiah 54:10).

In December 2008, I was on a plane with my family. As we hit a patch of intense turbulence, I heard the words of God in my heart say, "The world is about to enter a storm like it has never known." I looked over to my children, who were at the time two and three. They were laughing because they thought they were on a ride, unaware of the dangers of the plane. Then the Lord said to my heart, "And this is how My church can ride the storm out, in peace and joy in My loving arms."

Jesus never said He would deliver us out of the storms of life. He actually said that in this life we would have troubles but that He had overcome the world. Everything that this world tries to throw at us is already overcome by Him. He promises peace (John 16:33)—peace and joy in the midst of every storm as we remain in Him (John 15:11). It is real, tangible peace and joy that aren't conditional on what we are experiencing, overcoming in every situation as we draw into Him.

At the onset of a storm that came to our lives a few years back in the form of a cancer diagnosis to my mom and me at the same time, the Lord spoke to my heart that cancer bows to the lordship of Jesus Christ. One day during this time, as we walked through this storm with that declaration filling our mouths, I felt led by the Lord to drive to the bay where we lived in Alaska. Resurrection Bay is surrounded by mountains on all sides. At all times, it is breathtakingly beautiful. Many days the waters are rough with many waves because of the wind. On this particular day, it was completely calm, still as glass. The Holy Spirit spoke to my heart and said, "This is a picture of the eye of the storm." The eye of the storm is the place of calm in any storm. Jesus is the eye of the storm. We draw into Him in the midst of the storms of life, and there is safety there. There is peace and joy to be experienced that is not dependent on our circumstances and can't be purchased with this world's currency of money. There is a peace that passes all our understanding, meaning we can have tangible peace that won't make sense to our natural minds, because it is only available through Christ as we draw near to Him. Invite the Holy Spirit to release that into your life in the midst of whatever you are facing. Let His living presence set your heart free to walk in His peace and joy.

These storms that come and are coming are not intended for destruction to His children but to break open hearts so childlike trust can be restored. God desires that our hearts be opened up to the eternal in new ways so our hearts can live in the kingdom reality of Luke 12:32, "Do not be afraid, little flock, for your Father has been pleased to give you the kingdom." He desires to teach us to live in such trust and confidence in His love and care, to teach our hearts that He delights to share His eternal kingdom with us, ready to provide for us everything we have need of, day by day. "Sell your possessions and give to the poor" (Luke 12:33). Not that He is going to say this to everyone, but are our hearts even open to hear these words if He did speak them to our hearts? "Provide purses for yourselves that will not wear out." A purse is a container to hold things. Purses are intended to carry what is valuable or important to us. Our hearts are intended to be containers, carrying Jesus as the pearl of great price.

> Listen, listen to me, and eat what is good, and your soul will delight in the richest of fare. Give ear and come to me; hear me, that your soul may live. I will make an everlasting covenant with you. (Isaiah 55:2)

This everlasting covenant is an unshakeable covenant. An oath has been given by God about Jesus: "The Lord has sworn and will not change his mind: 'You are a priest forever'" (Hebrews 7:21). Because of this oath, Jesus has become the guarantee of a better covenant (Hebrews 7:22). Jesus is becoming our security and safety in reality, so we no longer need to draw on any earthly thing to bring us comfort or a sense of security. God is raising up a royal priesthood from out of this everlasting covenant of the new covenant of Jesus Christ. As they are hidden in Christ and rooted in His eternal love, this royal priesthood is receiving so much value from God in the secret place and are learning to trust in their Father's provision at all times, for all things. The storms that come only strengthen their hearts in His love and goodness as they keep their hearts open to Him and eyes on Him and remain seated with Him, listening to Him, obeying His voice, drawing from His peace and joy in the time of trouble.

In every situation and at all times, the Holy Spirit is continually returning the focus of the heart to the starting and finishing point of all things: Jesus Christ and His finished work on the cross born out of love, which is the fuel for all things. Because Jesus lives forever, He has a permanent priesthood. Therefore, He is able to save completely those who come to God through Him, because He always lives to intercede for them (Hebrews 7:24–25).

Jesus lives forever, making intercession that saves completely. In the secret place, we come to sit with Him, to worship Him, to hear His intercessions, to join in with His prayers that save completely in every situation.

Because Christ is alive and making intercession, there is a royal priesthood arising, being saved completely by the work of the Holy Spirit releasing Christ's love and life to every broken place in their lives. This is causing their hearts to live free.

Because Christ is alive and making intercession, there is a royal priesthood arising, hidden with Christ, living free and releasing Christ's intercessions that *save completely* into the earth by the power of His Spirit.

An Opening—the Curtain That Is His Body

Chapter 2 of Hebrews speaks to Jesus being made like us so He could join us to His glory through His suffering and death.

> In bringing many sons to glory, it was fitting that God, for whom and through whom everything exists, should make the author of their salvation perfect through

suffering. Both the one who makes men holy and those who are made holy are of the same family.

We have been brought into a new family. We have a perfect Father, and His Son has become the door for us to come in to this relationship. Hebrews gives us understanding that God desires sons who share in His glory. A whole new reality gets opened up to our hearts as we begin to see what Christ is inviting us into. No longer are we satisfied with knowing theological concepts of His words in Hebrews but the living reality of His presence in our hearts opening up these truths so we can find life in them that transforms us and then transforms everything around us. His beauty and His holiness attract us to Him, and we come closer. We enter into living from another reality. We enter into the glory of the new covenant. The glory of God is going to fill the whole earth. Let the glory of Christ in your heart begin to grow and then begin to spill out to those around you.

Everything that we see in Hebrews that Christ did to open the heavens is intended to be lived out for the world around us to experience His life and light. We are not only a people waiting for His second coming for Him to be revealed; we are expecting His love and life to be revealed and demonstrated right now. His beautiful body became the opening for which this is now possible.

> Therefore, brothers, since we have confidence to enter the Most Holy Place by the blood of Jesus, *by a new and living way opened for us through the curtain, that is, his body.* (Hebrews 10:19-20)

An opening has been made between heaven and earth. Through His death on the cross, Jesus became the opening, the open door. He is the door of access that no one can shut over your life to the kingdom and to His kingdom plans being released over your life. The revelation of Jesus, the son of man, who is the Christ, is the rock on which the church is built. His church is being built up and strengthened as they encounter Christ and His finished work in a deeper measure.

His people are going through the open door and keys to His kingdom are being given. There is increasing revelation that is coming of His kingdom that we are presently a part of, so the ways of this world can fall off of us. It is a kingdom that has one King, and the beauty of that kingdom is released through those who know their king and are being transformed because they have seen the beauty of His holiness. The revelation of this King who is a high priest forever in the order of Melchizedek (Hebrews 5:10) is opened up. Jesus, the High Priest, has met every requirement. He is holy, blameless, pure, set apart from sinners, exalted above the heavens, and being revealed to hearts. The new covenant of His love is being accessed.

The King's way is the way of love opened up to us and the world around us. Jesus, because His heart longed to honor His father and bring many sons into the glory that He shares with His father, broke open the heavens by becoming our great High Priest and by becoming the perfect sacrifice.

The Perfect High Priest—Let Us Draw Near

> For we do not have a high priest who is unable to sympathize with our weaknesses, but we have one who has been tempted in every way, just as we are- yet was without sin. Let us then approach the throne of grace with confidence, so that we may receive mercy and find grace to help us in our time of need. (Hebrews 4:15)

He knows our weaknesses. He isn't looking for us to be strong in ourselves, to buck up and do this thing. He understands that we are human and that we are weak, no matter how strong an exterior we try to put up. We have a High Priest who has sympathy for us, who feels what we are feeling and wants to help. We come near to Him (approach the throne of grace) so we can receive what we need, mercy and grace to strengthen our hearts.

> Since we have a great priest over the house of God, let us draw near to God with a sincere heart in full assurance of faith, having our hearts sprinkled to cleanse us from a guilty conscience. (Hebrews 10:21)

Jesus, our great High Priest, wants to give mercy and grace in our time of need, and He is wanting to cleanse our guilty conscience as we draw near in faith in who He is and what He has done. Our minds and hearts need to be washed, we are guilty, but there is freedom in His presence. There are promises in the above verses that are waiting to be laid hold of. Since we have a great priest over the house of God, let us draw near to God. He is inviting us to come close. He is not a high priest only serving once a year to make atonement for sin. He is always available, ready to apply His sacrifice for you.

> But when this priest had offered for all time one sacrifice for sins, he sat down at the right hand of God … Since that time he waits for his enemies to be made his footstool, because by one sacrifice he has made perfect forever those who are being made holy. (Hebrews 10:11–14)

"By one sacrifice, His sacrifice, He has made perfect forever." There's no need for other sacrifices. The work is complete. We leave striving to earn anything from God and enter into resting in Christ's love.

We leave striving to enter into the Father's presence. Christ's sacrifice is enough. He is the source of eternal salvation. We enter into the rest from striving in our own strength to overcome the power of sin in our own hearts and in the world around us. Our hearts coming to yield to the power of His love.

Through Jesus's perfect offering, we are being made holy. There is no other need for any sacrifice from our lives to establish holiness. Perfection has come. At this revelation, perfectionism has to go from our hearts. By one sacrifice, His sacrifice, He has made perfect forever those who are being made holy. Performing for God to become holy, or to keep everything held together, or trying to clear our consciences by doing "good" acts, or for man's approval to earn recognition, has to go from our lives. We can stop striving to be perfect. Our becoming holy comes from being joined to Him. He gives freely what is lacking. He makes up the difference. His holiness freely given to us strengthens our hearts and awakens destiny. Through His perfect sacrifice, we are set free to pursue Him in love and simply obey Him. We are set free to give Him what He wants.

> The point of what we are saying is this: We do have such a high priest, who sat down at the right hand of the throne of the Majesty in heaven, and who serves in the sanctuary, the true tabernacle set up by the Lord, not by man. (Hebrews 8:1–2)

His present position is He is sitting down. This means His work is done. Everything that needs to be done has been done. He is now serving that work to hearts that draw near. The only thing left is for our hearts to enter into rest because of the completeness of His work to save and purify us. We can stop striving to produce works for Him.

> There remains then, a Sabbath-rest for the people of God; for anyone who enters God's rest also rests from his own work, just as God did from his. Let us, therefore, make every effort to enter that rest, so that no one will fall by following their example of disobedience. (Hebrews 4:9)

A prophetic word: Come rest. Jesus Christ already did it. Come live in His love, find rest for your soul. Be weaned to live in rest (Psalm 131). Let us cease to produce in our own flesh works for God. Cut these off, that we may bring forth the life of God, not by might or power, but by His Holy Spirit.

This rest He calls us to live in will not mean that we will do nothing. In this rest that He calls us into, we begin to live in His fullness. Many of us, growing up in an American society of performance and achievement, have been trained from very young ages to produce and achieve. We are taught to resist being weak or needy. Embracing our lack apart from Him will be required to enter in to His fullness. There must be a deprogramming of our hearts and minds from the American way so we can enter into the King's way. Our hearts and minds are in need of training to be brought to stillness from activity, to be still and know that He is God. We learn to wait on Him to move and to not rush out ahead of Him in our anxiousness of heart. His Holy Spirit is present with us to teach our hearts to abide in Him, to live in rest and from rest, so that His life can released from our lives.

This rest that He calls us into is what releases true faith. This rest that He calls us to releases the activity of the Holy Spirit. We look at what He did so that faith can rise in our hearts to believe for the reality of those things to be awakened in us and released through us by the power of His Spirit flowing from us.

> Therefore, since we have a great high priest who has gone through the heavens, Jesus, the son of God, let us hold firmly to the faith we profess. (Hebrews 4:14)

We have a High Priest like no other priest—one who opened up the heavens by coming to earth, one who became the perfect sacrifice to restore us back to fellowship with God, offering His blood as the eternal sacrifice for our sin. He is the one who defeated death and was raised back to life, going back into heaven. He now sits at God's right hand, applying His perfect work for us in intercession (Hebrews 7:25). Let us look at what the Bible says about Jesus, our great High Priest, and begin to saturate ourselves in the reality of these truths, so that faith can rise up in our hearts to lay hold of all He has made available through His work on the cross. Let the Holy Spirit do His work in your heart. This revelation of Jesus Christ alive in our hearts as our eternal High Priest produces faith that comes from hearing God's word about what Christ has accomplished for us. From this faith awakened in our hearts, the Holy Spirit is present with us to release His power to stand and contend in prayer for the promises of God revealed for our own lives and for others. Hebrews 11:1 says that faith is being sure of what we hope for, certain of what we do not see. You don't need to "see" things in the natural to believe them.

He desires to give us eyes that see by faith what He is doing. Since we have a great high priest who has gone back into heaven, let us draw near and hold firm to His promises, no matter what the opposition in our own hearts or in the world around us. This is where faith that is professed becomes true, living faith.

An Assignment from God

All of God's plans begin in His own heart. Every high priest is selected from among men and is appointed to represent them in matters related to God (Hebrews 5:1). In Christ's day, the high priestly office was in the hands of a family that had bought control of the position. The appointment of this office had strayed far from the original plan. Hebrews 5:4–5 states, "No one takes this honor upon himself; he must be called by God. So Christ also did not take upon himself the glory of becoming a high priest." In the next passage, God said to him, "You are my Son; today I have become your Father" (Hebrews 5:5). Through these verses, God is affirming the truth that Christ is His Son and is linking His sonship to the priestly calling.

Christ lived to do His Father's will because He loved to do His Father's will. He was not looking for a position. These verses tell us the Father assigned Christ as the eternal High Priest. Christ willingly accepted His Father's plan. He didn't grab it for Himself. He was secure in His identity as a Son.

As we daily live being fed by the love of our Father, our hearts begin to live in the identity of who we are as children of God. Our hearts begin to turn from an earthly perspective of external striving for position and recognition and begin to live in the peace and rest that children know when they are safe in their Father's arms and are loved by their Father.

> How great is the love the Father has lavished on us, that we should be called children of God! (1 John 3:1)

We can't grasp the extent of this love He longs to lavish on us with our minds. The depth of this love can only be revealed to our hearts by the Holy Spirit's work. The revelation of this love daily given to our hearts leads us into living from this greater reality that we are His children, called to be a part of His royal priesthood.

This new covenant has a permanent priesthood and Jesus is the High Priest of this covenant, bringing forth sons of God being joined to His Father's glory and who serve as priests of the Lord in the earth.

This royal priesthood is resting in the strength and power of what Jesus purchased through His death and resurrection. This royal priesthood is arising to release the resurrection life of Christ, the new and living way that has been opened up to us.

A New Way

> Therefore, brothers, since we have confidence to enter the Most Holy Place by the blood of Jesus, by a *new* and *living* way opened for us. (Hebrew 10:19–20)

The writer of the book of Hebrews explains that even under the old covenant, the shedding of blood was required for the cleansing of sin, and without blood there is no forgiveness. Under the old covenant, the blood required for sin was from bulls and goats. Every year, the high priest had to enter the most holy place with blood for that year's sins for the nation of Israel.

Under the new covenant, we enter freely into God's presence through the blood of Jesus, a new and living way that has been opened up for us.

> he entered heaven itself, now to appear for us in God's presence. Nor did he enter heaven to offer himself again, and again, the way the high priest enters the Most Holy Place every year with blood ... so Christ was sacrificed once to take away the sins of many people. (Hebrews 9:24-28)

God loves to make all things new. He loves to transform the old way into a new way. Isaiah prophesies a new thing (Isaiah 42:9). Jeremiah declares a time that would come for a new covenant. (Jeremiah 31:31–33). Jesus spoke in Matthew of a new wineskin and a new wine, and His death opened up a new way:

> If perfection could have been attained through the Levitical priesthood, why was there still need for another priest to come—one in the order of Melchizedek, not in the order of Aaron? (Hebrews 7:11)

This states simply that this new way that brought perfection and a new order of priests came, not in the "proper" order but in a totally unexpected way. Under the old covenant, priests could only serve from out of the tribe of Levi, in the order of Aaron. The above verses tell us that Jesus's new covenant priesthood is in the order of Melchizedek.

Genesis 14 tells the account of Melchizedek, the king of Salem. After Abram defeated the enemy and rescued Lot, Melchizedek showed up to serve him bread and wine and to bless Abram. Hebrews 7 also speaks of who Melchizedek was, with Hebrews 7:1 describing him as king of Salem and priest of God Most High. He blessed Abram, and then Abram gave him a tenth of everything. He is described in these verses as his name meaning "king of righteousness" and king of Salem meaning "king of peace," both titles that the Bible uses to describe Jesus. Jesus's priesthood is in the order of Melchizedek, one that is both kingly and priestly. The prophetic symbolism of Melchizedek, a priestly king, serving the bread and wine to Abram and blessing Him, points to Jesus also.

Jesus's statement about himself in John 6:35 was that He was the bread of life. "He who comes to me will never go hungry, and he who believes in me will never be thirsty." Jesus has living bread and new wine to give. We enter His priestly ministry as we are fed by Him. As we feed on His life, we in turn have His life to give.

"For when there is a change of the priesthood, there must also be a change of the law" (Hebrews 7:12). These verses state that when there is a change of priesthood, there is also a change of the law. The priesthood changes, and the law changes. Perfection is coming with this new priesthood. Perfect love casts out all fear (1 John 4:18). The law gives way to the law of love (Matthew 22:36–40). When perfection comes, the imperfect disappears (1 Corinthians 13:9–12). This Melchizedek priesthood brings perfection and the ability to gaze upon Him and to know even as we are known (2 Corinthians 3:18). There is more to be revealed to our hearts.

"The Lord has sworn and will not change his mind; You are a priest forever, in the order of Melchizedek" (Psalm 110).

Perfection couldn't be obtained through the old order priesthood, so midway through the serving of this priesthood, God began to speak of another priesthood, a kingly priesthood, a new way that would be opened up. This psalm of David, written 1044 years before Christ, revealed God's plan that Jesus would come through David's kingly line, the tribe of Judah.

> He of whom these things are said belonged to a different tribe, and no one from that tribe has ever served at the altar. For it is clear that our Lord descended from Judah, and in regard to that tribe Moses said nothing about priests. And what we have said is even more clear if another priest like Melchizedek appears, one who has become a priest not on the basis of a regulation as to His ancestry but on the basis of the power of an indestructible life. (Hebrews 7:14–16)

You are called to a royal priesthood established on the basis of the power of Christ's indestructible life and the power of His love. Jesus came through the tribe of Judah. Moses spoke nothing about priests coming through that tribe. Just as Moses and the law gave no indicator of how the promised Messiah and new order of priests would come, there is nothing in your past that can either qualify you or disqualify you from this priestly calling. You don't have to have the "right" pedigree, get voted into, or buy a place into this priesthood. None of these things will qualify you for a place in this priesthood.

Jesus fulfilled all the requirements of this priesthood, becoming the *eternal* priest in the order of Melchizedek as He completed the work on the cross and was raised to life.

Don't let your mind shut down at those words. We will not be like the generation the writer of Hebrews was speaking to when he wrote, "We have much to say about this, but it is hard to explain because you are slow to learn" (Hebrews 5:11). This generation will enter into all that is available in Christ. The *Webster's Dictionary* defines the word *indestructible* as "not able to be destroyed." I believe there is an expediting by the Spirit to leave the elementary things and move into maturity in Christ as the word is opened up to see Christ and the indestructible nature of His work and the power of His love that shatters the powers of the most formidable strongholds of darkness.

This Melchizedek priesthood has kingdom authority to release the perfection and fullness of God's plans. We will look at this in a later chapter. For now, I will simply say the way we can have Christ's authority to see these strongholds of darkness demolished in our time is to be joined to Him as the branch is joined to the vine, the one from whom true life flows.

There is a royal priesthood arising, living in Christ, the new and living way. This new covenant priesthood is called to serve the living bread and new wine of His presence. They are releasing the blessings of heaven to others.

Living Way

Hebrews 1:2 states that God, in these last days, speaks through His Son. As we listen to His words, His all-powerful, all-sustaining words, we receive His life in our hearts by the work of the Holy Spirit and are released to receive the fullness of what He has accomplished for us.

"The Son is the radiance of God's glory and the exact representation of His being, sustaining all things by Your powerful word" (Hebrews 1:3). All things are sustained. The *Webster's Dictionary* definition of the word *sustained* means "to keep in existence." He is life. There is not life apart from Him. His powerful word is in our hearts, continually feeding newness of life to us. If His words are the only source of true life as Hebrews 1 declares, how can we not be found listening to His words?

A royal priesthood is arising in the earth, being fully satisfied by Jesus, the giver of life, and this royal priesthood is being joined to Him in all things. Jesus's words to us in John 6:57 are this: "Just as the living Father sent Me and I live because of the Father, so the one who feeds on Me will live because of Me." We are a priesthood whose lives revolve around Jesus. We eat His words for life, and we eat His flesh as we obey His living word.

Our sole purpose in being is Jesus. We are a royal priesthood living continually in His presence—a royal priesthood arising, eating the bread of His presence and feasting on the new wine of His Spirit. We enter into the discipleship that Jesus calls His followers to in John 6:54. His ways have not changed to become more relevant for the American culture. "I tell you the truth, unless you eat the flesh of the Son of Man and drink his blood, you have no life in you."

Haven't we tried to be joined to Him *and* be joined to things that have no eternal purpose long enough? Isn't it time for Holy separation unto Him and His eternal purposes? Isn't it time for our hearts to be wholly surrendered to Him even as the physical picture of the Old Testament priests binding gold plates to their foreheads inscribed with the words, "Holy to the Lord" becomes a living reality in us and we become wholly His?

Hearts are being wholly restored by the new and living way that has been opened up. A tidal wave of His Spirit is released through a priestly army joined to their High Priest of the new covenant. Jesus's declaration that from our bellies would flow rivers of living water is becoming a reality.

Jesus, Our Eternal High Priest, Releasing a Multitude of Priests to Arise

In the book of Jeremiah, there is a prophetic promise given many years before Christ's coming. The fulfillment of this promise would be found in Jesus Christ and through a multitude of new covenant priests that would arise and shine from out of His eternal covenant:

> In those days and at that time I will make a righteous Branch sprout from David's line; He will do what is just and right in the land. In those days Judah will be saved and Jerusalem will live in safety. This is the name by which it will be called: The Lord our righteousness. For this is what the Lord says: David will never fail to have a man to sit on the throne of the house of Israel, nor will the priests, who are Levites, ever fail to have a man to

stand before me continually to offer burnt offerings, to burn grain offerings and to present sacrifices. The word of the Lord came to Jeremiah: This is what the Lord says: If you can break my covenant with the day and my covenant with the night, so that day and night no longer come at their appointed time, then my covenant with David my servant- and my covenant with the Levites who are priests ministering before me- can be broken and David will no longer have a descendant to reign on his throne. *I will make the descendants of David my servant and the Levites who minister before me as countless as the stars of the sky and as measureless as the sand on the seashore.* (Jeremiah 33:15–22)

Our God is so loving and kind. Even in the face of impending judgment brought on by disobedience of His chosen people, He is speaking restoration. He speaks of an unshakeable commitment to His word by providing all that is needed to fulfill the word. These passages speak of the ultimate fulfillment of these promises through Jesus. Out of Jesus's eternal covenant of love that He fashioned at the cross, an eternal priesthood arises. Jesus's kingly and priestly authority were prophesied through these passages in Jeremiah and fulfilled at the cross, releasing a priesthood that is as vast as the sand of the sea-shores. It is a royal priesthood hidden in Christ, revealing Christ's kingly and priestly authority in the earth.

Out of the ashes of man's failure, we see God continually declaring that He is the restorer of all things. There is no desolate place He is unable to renew and restore.

3

The Unveiling

But their minds were made dull, for to this day the
same veil remains when the old covenant is read.
It has not been taken away. Even to this day when
Moses is read, a veil covers their hearts. But whenever
anyone turns to the Lord, the veil is taken away.

2 Corinthians 3:14

The *Webster's* definition of the word *veil* means "a concealing curtain" or "something that hides or obscures." The word *curtain* is defined as "a device that conceals or acts as a barrier."

The Old Testament priest went behind the veil once a year, to make atonement for sin. Moses had to put a veil over his face to hide the glory on him after being with God. Both pictures became constant reminders to the Israelites that there were restrictions on the presence of God. Both became pictures that the glory of God was only accessible at certain periods of time. There was a barrier between God and man.

To see our true calling in Christ as priests of the Lord, any veils over our hearts and minds must be removed. Second Corinthians 3 does not speak only to the unbeliever who has not seen Christ in His glory for salvation, but it speaks to every heart of an ever-increasing glory in this new covenant and of an unveiling that allows us to see Him till we are transformed.

The words of verse 13 spring up in my heart as I write these definitions. "We are not like Moses who put a veil over his face to keep the Israelites from gazing at it while the radiance was fading away." As a royal priesthood, we are not called to conceal the glory of God on our lives; we are called to live unveiled, beholding Him. We are called to live unveiled, reflecting His radiance.

> And we, who with unveiled faces all reflect the Lord's glory, are being transformed into his likeness with ever-increasing glory, which comes from the Lord, who is the Spirit. (2 Corinthians 3:18)

These verses in 2 Corinthians always gripped my heart as I would read them, knowing there was hidden glory on these words that my mind could not connect with but that my spirit thrived in. What did it mean to reflect with an unveiled face the Lord's glory? It caused me to question if there were there still veils on my heart that prevented me from clearly seeing Him. Were there still veils on my heart that kept His glory hidden over my life?

When we study the Old Testament priesthood, we see people receiving from man on behalf of God. In the priesthood of the Old Covenant, the people have no direct access to God. We see the priests ministering to the people on a different level than the people. Their primary ministry is to the people. The priests have very limited access to God and only at prescribed times. The high priest was only allowed access into the holy of holies once a year. All of this paints the picture of very limited access. The veil is still in place. We need to consider, are we still living out of this old covenant reality, where we only believe we can access God's presence at certain times, or in certain places?

When Christ died, Matthew 27:51 says that the natural veil in the temple in Israel was torn from top to bottom. God tore the veil as a sign of what was happening in the spirit realm. At Christ's death, the veil concealing God's weighty glory was removed. The presence of God was opened up to all, at all times.

Salvation is intended to restore fellowship. Some come to Christ but then stay in mind-sets that actually feed old beliefs that they are separated from God, rejected by Him, that God is distant. They are more comfortable with an idea of going to another person to hear from God as fear keeps them still bound from drawing near to Him. Others are more comfortable with keeping the people coming to them, so they don't have to deal with the issues of their own hearts. Still others just don't know there is full access available.

This was the reality I had functioned in for years, receiving Christ but continuing to live out of mind-sets of rejection and shame and performance that limited my sense of access to Him. I had knowledge in my head of God but was not experiencing His life-giving touch upon my heart. I knew about God and worked to earn intimacy with Him, not realizing what was already freely available, continuing to live in a reality where God seemed unapproachable. His acceptance seemed impossible.

He is calling us to live with our hearts and minds unveiled, to step into His love and move deeper and deeper into His glory by the power of the Spirit. A spirit of religion creates a veil that causes us to fear drawing near to Him. The spirit of grace on our hearts causes us to draw near in faith and trust that He loves and desires us and has done everything to have relationship with us. There is also an unveiling of the word to see more clearly what has been opened up. All of His words to us are there to be experienced.

> Now the Lord is the Spirit, and where the Spirit of the
> Lord is, there is freedom. (2 Corinthians 3:17)

If we view the word through a lens of religion, distant from God, "self" needing to improve itself, we will always feel condemned. Our lives will be filled with striving to perform some work to bring to

Him. Sitting with Him to gaze on Him and be transformed will not be a focus for us. There will be no time to rest and wait in His presence. There is too much to be done. God will feel like a taskmaster. For some, it isn't that they don't have a heart for God; it just seems too hard, so they give up and just walk away from God altogether.

If we view the word through the finished work of the cross, we will be empowered by the Holy Spirit to die to self and live in Christ and be fully restored. We will see Christ doing everything to wash us and restore us. We will open our hearts wide to His transforming gaze. We can experience the ever-increasing glory of the new covenant as the Holy Spirit brings freedom to our hearts.

The Holy Spirit is with us to help our minds be fully opened to see this gospel, "the light of the gospel of the glory of Christ, who is the image of God" (2 Corinthians 4:6). This gospel of His glory renews and regenerates us by His love, at all times, in all situations. David Ravenhill, author and speaker, describes the glory of God in a simple and powerful way. He says the glory of God is the nature of God.

The most common word for *glory* is the Hebrew word *kabod*, meaning "heavy in weight." In the New Testament, the Greek word for glory is *doxazo*, meant to convey a sense of brilliance or radiance.

Ephesians 5:25 encourages us that it is God's nature to share Himself with us.

> Christ loved the church and gave himself up for her to make her holy, cleansing her by the washing with water through the word, and to present her to himself as a radiant church, without stain or wrinkle or any other blemish but holy and blameless.

God's end goal for transformation of His people is into a radiant church, a bride without spot or wrinkle. He is purifying a bride who is being washed with the water of His word, becoming radiant. There are real things that He needs to wash from our lives: fear, shame, rejection, unbelief. These veils block our seeing Him and reflecting Him. To become what we are called to become, we will live unveiled, beholding Him.

His bride radiates His nature in the earth, a reflection of His glory.

In His glory, there is a restoration of all things. We can look back to the beginning to see God's original intention for us. "The man and his wife were both naked, and they felt no shame" (Genesis 2:25). Nothing is blocking the fellowship. No veil. No shame. The writings of Genesis share the story of intimacy and deep fellowship with God as they walked with God in the cool of the day. We read further and see what sin introduced.

> Then the eyes of them were opened, and they realized they were naked; so they sewed fig leaves together and made coverings for themselves. Then they heard the sound of the Lord God as he was walking the garden in the cool of the day, and they hid from the Lord God among the trees of the garden. But the Lord God called to the man, "Where are you?" He answered, "I heard you in the garden, and I was afraid because I was naked; so I hid." (Genesis 3:8–10)

As soon as sin entered, man began to hide. Fig leaves were sewn together to hide their condition. Jesus died, and the literal veil in the temple was torn. The spiritual veil over men's hearts was also torn. The rejection that sin brought in the garden was defeated, and we could come again to live before Him, close and protected. As we looked at in chapter 2, Jesus has become the curtain. The veil of separation has been removed, and the new and living way has been opened up through the curtain of Jesus's body and we are being hidden in Him. It is now safe to become vulnerable. We can stop hiding from Him. God is removing the walls of self-protection around our hearts so we can live in His light and under His shade of protection, resting in His shadow, unafraid.

To enter into our calling as priests of the new covenant, the fig leaves of shame and fear will be removed. In Leviticus 8:5, when Moses brought Aaron and his sons forward to ordain them as priests, he washed them with water and then clothed them.

He comes to wash us with the word of any residual effects of the Old Covenant and clothe us in His surpassing glory.

> Now if the ministry that brought death, which was engraved in letters on stone, came with glory, so that the Israelites could not look steadily at the face of Moses because of its glory, fading though it was, will not the ministry of the Spirit be even more glorious?... For what was glorious has no glory now in comparison with the surpassing glory. And if what was fading away came with glory, how much greater is the glory of that which lasts! (2 Corinthians 3:7–11)

David, a man after God's heart, penned the words in Psalm 139:23 that expressed a cry for God to, "Search me, and know my heart; "Test me and know my anxious thoughts. See if there is any offensive way in me, and lead me in the way everlasting." God knew David's heart. David was desiring his own heart fully exposed to the loving gaze of His Savior, so He could be led into freedom. We move into a place of trust as we open wide our hearts to His beautiful gaze. In His gaze, the veils of rejection, fear, and shame that we all have carried or still carry are removed. The ministry of His Spirit on our hearts is glorious.

To live wide open in our hearts, we will have to follow our Lord's command to become childlike, totally trusting, and without pretense. One morning, while working on this chapter, I was bike riding with my daughter, Anna, who was eight at the time. I was reminded of something that happened the night before that was a picture to me of living unveiled. I did not see it in the moment, but in the morning air, watching my daughter on her bike, I saw it clearly.

The previous evening, I sat at my computer to do some writing, feeling mired down by life's challenges, veils covering my heart that kept me from seeing Him. I wanted to press through so I could continue writing. I was asking Him for clarity. My wonderful daughter came into the room and sat down at the desk where a computer sits. She began to work on something, and I asked her what she was doing. She declared that she was working on her book about chipmunks from around the world. There was no sense of burden in this task, only joy and an expectancy that she could do anything. (This is a regular occurrence for Anna, starting a new book about a variety of subjects.) That night, for the first time, I told her that I was also working on a book. Her eyes grew wide with wonder that we were working on the same thing.

Children are amazing. They believe there are no limitations on what they can do. Life is just waiting to be laid hold of. In her mind, there is no reason why she can't write a book. That is the beauty of watching believing, childlike faith before my eyes, no veils or limitations, just radiating the glory of God. Seeing this encouraged my heart to press past the veil of unbelief and open wide my heart, see God, and believe Him for what He was doing.

Jesus said of a childlike heart that it would unveil the kingdom to our hearts.

> I praise you, Father, Lord of heaven and earth, because you have hidden these things from the wise and learned, and revealed them to little children. Yes, Father, for this was your good pleasure. (Matthew 11:25–26)

What are the secrets of the kingdom that are still veiled to you? Where is there access to God's presence that still feels closed to your heart? Where is there a veil that still conceals the glory God intends to release from your life: veils of religion, shame, rejection, fear of man, unbelief, deceitfulness through sin?

Matthew 13 is the parable of the sower and the invitation to sow and reap without measure. The disciples came and asked Jesus why he veiled his words in verse 10, "Why do you speak to the people in parables?" Jesus responded that it was the hardening of man's heart, not the desire of His heart to do so. In verse 12, Jesus shares His heart to give more and more, until there is an abundance. He replied, "The knowledge of the secrets of the Kingdom of heaven has been given to you, but not to them. Whoever has will be given more, and he will have an abundance" (Matthew 13:12).

May this generation not be like the generation that Hebrews 3 speaks of, a generation that, because of unbelief, turned away from God, who is described as living (Hebrews 3:12) and did not enter into the fullness of His promises. I believe God wants to recalibrate our hearts as He leads us in casting off those things that hinder us from fully gazing upon Jesus. Eyes and hearts are locked on Him in an "accurate and exact way" as the mark. May this generation turn toward Him to gaze on Him, be transformed by Him, and reflect His glory in our times.

At the turn of the twenty-first century at Azusa Street, the glory of the Lord was unveiled in a fresh way to a small group of people. It transformed them and drew others, and they in turn began to bring the transformative power of Jesus Christ to the nations, not by might or power, but by the Spirit's power. Accounts from the Azusa Street revival tell of God's glory that rested on the mission and could be seen from a distance at night and tell how after a year of God's outpouring, crutches lined the walls where the meetings were held, left by people who had been healed in the glory.

There is a promise that to whomever has, more will be given. There is a promise of ever-increasing glory to be laid hold of. There is glory to be unlocked in the hearts of God's people that will bring transformation everywhere they go.

"Arise, shine for your light has come and the glory of the Lord rises upon you."

As we behold him and are transformed by Him, we will arise to shine, reflecting Him as the glory of the Lord is released from our lives. There is a fresh release of His glory to be unveiled for the world to encounter in these times. When Jesus, standing at the tomb of Lazarus, told them to take away the stone, Martha exclaimed that he had been dead for four days and there would be an odor. Jesus's response to her was, "Did I not tell you that if you believed, you would see the glory of God?" (John 11:38–40).

There is resurrection life released in the glory He is unveiling from your life. He is calling hearts to arise and shine in the growing darkness, with the stench of death all around. The veil of fear that keeps hearts from arising to go are removed in the gazing on Him. We don't have to fear the odor of death. With Christ, death gives way to resurrection life.

There is a royal priesthood that is arising, having the Son revealed to their hearts, and from this revelation of the Son, they long to see the Son revealed. "Christ in you, the Hope of Glory" (Colossians 1:27). Christ is the only hope for the times we live in. When we come to Christ, we are reborn and are given a new nature, the very nature of Christ. His glory is given to us. His nature is being reflected through your life as you live by His Spirit.

The Holy Spirit is present with us to lead us to rise up past the veils of opposition that are in us and around us and shine His life and light in the growing darkness. These verses in 2 Corinthians 4:7 illustrate the picture of Christ living in us by His Spirit. "But we have this treasure in jars of clay to show that this all-surpassing power is from God and not from us." He is the treasure. The power comes from Him. We hold him in these jars of clay, these earthen vessels. The next verses share a secret to the unveiling of His glory from our lives, so we reflect Him:

> We are hard pressed on every side, but not crushed, perplexed, but not in despair; persecuted, but not abandoned; struck down, but not destroyed. We always carry around in our body the death of Jesus, so that the life of Jesus may also be revealed in our body. For we who are alive are always being given over to death for Jesus' sake so that his life may be revealed in our mortal body. So then, death is at work in us, but life is at work in you.

We press past the pressures and the setbacks we encounter. We keep our eyes fixed on Him, and we do not shrink back from His fiery gaze of love and holiness on our hearts. His death is being worked in us so that His life can be released through us. The unveiling of His glory is the life of Jesus revealed. The glory of God is revealed, his very weighty, radiating nature, through His people who are living unveiled.

John 2 shares the story of Jesus's first miracle, where He turned the water into wine from out of stone water jars, the kind used in ceremonial washing. "We have this treasure in jars of clay." Priests are being washed with the water of the word. The water was turned into wine.

> The master of the banquet tasted the water that had been turned into wine. He did not realize where it had come from, though the servants who had drawn the water knew. Then he called the bridegroom aside and said, "Everyone brings out the choice wine first and then the cheaper wine after the guests have had too much to drink; but you have saved the best till now." This, the first of his miraculous signs, Jesus performed at Cana in Galilee. He thus revealed his glory, and his disciples put their faith in him. (John 2:9–11)

God has saved the best for last: a Melchizedek priesthood, arising to serve the new wine of His Spirit that He has prepared for this generation. Priests of the new covenant are broken open, revealing His glory. God is calling and equipping a Melchizedek priesthood to release the miracles of Jesus. There is a harvest of lives changed as they encounter His glory and put their faith and trust in Him.

> He has made us competent as ministers of a new covenant—not of the letter but of the Spirit; for the letter kills but the Spirit gives life. (2 Corinthians 3:6)

4

A Hidden Priesthood

Since, then, you have been raised with Christ, set your
hearts on things above, where Christ is seated at the
right hand of God. Set your minds on things above,
not on earthly things. For you died, and your life is
now hidden with Christ in God.

Colossians 3:1-3

God is calling His church to arise and shine in the growing darkness. There is a royal priesthood in the order of Melchizedek, who are finding Christ as their life and are discovering Him in His priestly and kingly authority over their hearts. Hearts are being opened up and enlarged by His love. They are being fed the bread of His presence and the new wine that He serves them as they draw into the secret place to sit with Christ. The Holy Spirit is really with us and in us, imparting these things to our hearts. In the hidden place with Christ, as we eat and drink of Him, our own strivings begin to die, earthly things that grip our focus lose their power, and our minds are lifted to a higher place of seeing, where

Christ is seated, in all His authority. Our hearts are being liberated to a life hidden in Christ. In God's economy, the way to hiddenness in Christ will lead us through the wilderness. The wilderness seasons that God takes us through is where we learn to depend solely on Him.

Into the Wilderness

The Bible tells a story of a man who left his system of influence to find favor with God in the desert. In Luke 1:5, the Bible states that John the Baptist was born to a priest named Zechariah, who belonged to the priestly division of Abijah; his wife Elizabeth was also a descendant of Aaron. John would not find his authority from the priestly courts of the old order, but as His father prophesied about him in Luke 1:76, he would "be called a prophet of the Most High; for you will go on before the Lord to prepare the way for him." He would leave the old order of priests to enter the new. He would go into the desert to receive his training. His diet would be locust and honey, his wardrobe camel's hair. He would leave his system of influence to find favor with God. He would be used of the Lord to prepare the people to receive Christ and a new day that was dawning on humankind. He would be raised up as a voice in the wilderness calling out to prepare hearts to receive Christ when He came. John the Baptist was the one Isaiah prophesied of,

> A voice of one calling in the desert prepare the way for the Lord, make straight in the wilderness a highway for our God ... And the glory of the Lord will be revealed, and all mankind together will see it. (Isaiah 40:3–5)

John's heart to decrease that Christ could increase is revealed in John 3:29–30:

> The bride belongs to the bridegroom. The friend who attends the bridegroom waits and listens for him, and is full of joy when he hears the bridegroom's voice. That joy is mine, and it is now complete. He must become greater; I must become less.

John lived with a cry in his heart for more of the kingdom of heaven and the voice of the bridegroom to be opened up to his generation.

In this hour, God is raising up a royal priesthood who, like John, have this cry in their hearts. They are longing for Christ to be revealed to their generation. They are embracing the wilderness seasons, to be hidden in Christ and joined to the ways of His Spirit. They are finding the ways of the Lord that appear foolish to their natural minds but are opening up God's highway. They are preparing the way of the Lord and releasing the glory of the latter house, bringing a harvest into Christ. Who will prepare the way for His coming? Where can He build His house?

As we are hidden in Christ and die to self, we are freed from pursuing the approval of man. Jesus had favor with God and men. His focus was on having favor with God. His favor among men was given by God. He did not pursue it. There is coming a royal priesthood who embrace the wilderness of hiddenness to find favor with God. In the secret place, they are finding their delight is in God alone and doing His will. In the secret place, they are receiving their approval from God, not from what they do for Him but because of who they are to Him. This is developing a strength in their hearts to stand with Him in His ways of bringing in the harvest into fullness in Christ.

Christ was born in a stable. He truly has no reputation that He is trying to hold on to. Maybe that is why he loves the weak, foolish things that so confound man's wisdom.

He truly doesn't care what anyone thinks. He isn't trying to impress anyone. He really does go after the one. To find Him, we have to go to where He sends us and be determined that our hearts want Him more than anything else. "If we seek Him, we will find Him, if we seek Him with all our hearts." Isn't that the quest the wise men of old went on and found him in an unlikely place and an unlikely form? Daniel 12:3 says, "Those who are wise will shine like the brightness of the heavens and lead many to righteousness." Should our pursuit not be to find true wisdom, and isn't He the hidden wisdom?

From Barrenness Comes Enlargement

> For my thoughts are not your thoughts, neither are
> your ways my ways, declares the Lord. As the heavens
> are higher than earth, so are my ways higher than your
> ways and my thoughts than your thoughts. (Isaiah
> 55:8–9)

The way God raised up John as a voice to his generation, or the way
Jesus would come, born lowly in a stable, is not how we would do
things. God doesn't think like us; His ways are not our ways. God is
raising up a people who will resist the cultures of the day that can be
found even in the church, to find God's ways.

There is a generation of priests being raised up with a cry in their
hearts for more. But it is not a soulish cry for more that the American
culture has known that sometimes feels like it has infiltrated the
church in America too deeply—more fries, more goods, more home,
more space, more ministry, more buildings. As they are hidden in
Christ, the cry that God is releasing in this generation of priests is a
cry for the hidden more, the enlarged place of the life of the Spirit.
The word *enlarged* in the dictionary means to make or become bigger,
more extensive. This priesthood that is arising is making room for the
Holy Spirit's work as they decrease so He can increase. They are
desiring to see a move of God that comes not by might or power but
by His Spirit.

When God called us to move to Alaska, we had come from
Omaha, Nebraska. There we had served at a church in a prayer
ministry. A verse on a wall in the prayer room there was Isaiah 54:2,
"Enlarge the place of your tent, stretch your tent curtains wide, do not
hold back; lengthen your cords, strengthen your stakes."

The literal interpretation of this verse speaks to a promise given
to Israel about an immediate deliverance from her captivity in
Babylon, but the ultimate fulfillment is through their Messiah, coming
to bring restoration at the return of Christ when He comes to set up
His millennial kingdom.

Does this mean we can only study the scripture for historical meaning, or does God have revelation from all of His word that can reveal who He is and have application for the times we live in? God's word, the whole Bible, is a book of continual discovery of the heart, purposes, and plans of God, revealing Christ in all things.

Second Timothy 3:16 says, "All Scripture is God-breathed and is useful for teaching, rebuking, correcting and training in righteousness." This means that every scripture God can use to instruct our hearts. We want to understand the literal meaning of Old Testament scripture but also be open to God's Spirit breathing upon His word to bring insight and revelation into our lives for the here and now. We never want to interpret the word to make it say what we want it to say. He is about bringing our hearts into full submission to His will and ways. We need the Holy Spirit's ministry as we study the word of God. We need a hunger to encounter Jesus as we read the word of God. We ask the Holy Spirit for understanding to interpret the very words of God. When our hearts our hungry for God, trusting not in what we think we know, God's Spirit will lead us into all truth concerning God's words. The Holy Spirit will breathe on the word with application for our times as we pray.

In my early years of living in Seward, Alaska, God began to turn my attention to the verse that preceded the above verse in Isaiah 54:2. As God began to open up these verses to my heart, He began to link this verse in Isaiah 54:1 as the necessary component to finding the fruitfulness of enlargement that Isaiah 54:2 speaks about. In these verses, God is promising a time of restoration and enlargement out of barrenness for Israel through restored relationship with God as their Maker and husband. I believe God is giving a key in these verses to unlock hope and a promise of restoration for our times as well.

> Sing, O barren woman, you who never bore a child; burst into song, shout for joy, you who were never in labor; because more are the children of the desolate woman than of her who has a husband, says the Lord. Enlarge the place of your tent, stretch your tent curtains wide, do not hold back; lengthen your cords, strengthen

your stakes, For you will spread out to the right and to the left; your descendants will dispossess nations and settle in their desolate cities. Do not be afraid; you will not suffer shame. Do not fear disgrace; you will not be humiliated. You will forget the shame of your youth... For your Maker is your husband. (Isaiah 54:1–5)

Paul, in the book of Galatians, refers to these same verses in 4:27 as he opens up the scriptures to the Galatians about two mothers, two covenants. One is the law that Galatians 4:24 says bears slaves. The other covenant is the new covenant of Jesus Christ and her children are free. One came forth through man's effort. The other is a result of a promise. This is the life of God that the Spirit births, bringing forth abundant fruit, children who are free in Christ, not slaves to religious performance and the law. In Galatians 4:19, Paul speaks to a labor as if he were in childbirth until Christ was formed in them.

To see the enlargement of His Spirit in a place, we must embrace the wilderness of barrenness. There is a promise in this verse in Isaiah 54:1 that the barren, desolate woman will bear more children. When I looked up the word *desolate* in the dictionary, it gave a definition as "in the state of bleak and dismal emptiness." It is not possible that life could come from this state of being desolate. In the natural, a desolate woman would not believe she had any hope of having children. In the natural, barren women are not singing and shouting for joy. God is pointing to a supernatural reality that gets opened up to those who will believe His promises and live by the Spirit. To enter into the enlarged place of the life of the Spirit and the harvest He brings from that place, He is calling hearts into the reality of living barren.

In the secret, hidden place with Christ, we encounter the barrenness of our own hearts to do His work apart from the Spirit's work. In the secret, hidden place with Christ, our hearts are enlarged to His love and His Spirit's work in and through our lives. As this happens, a determination to live barren to accomplishing anything in our own strength for God and to live alive to His Spirit's work, joined to Him in His work and ways, begins to grow and deepen.

Again, the wilderness is where God weans His people from other sources of dependency so they will trust only in Him, looking only to Him for all things. Psalm 131:2 makes a beautiful declaration, "I have stilled and quieted my soul; like a weaned child with its mother, like a weaned child is my soul within me." As we embrace the wilderness seasons and the weaning process God brings into our lives, our hearts are brought into rest and trust in His way to do His work, trusting only in the Spirit for this work to be accomplished.

The truth is, we are barren to being able to produce anything of eternal value apart from His living presence. We no longer need to try to add to His work, no longer have to mask that truth. We can embrace it. There is abundant joy and a song released in our hearts that spring forth from death to self. We are like children, weak and so needy for Him. He desires relationship with us, deep intimacy. He wants to wean hearts into rest from religious performance, so His Spirit can be released to move and work.

In the secret, hidden place with Christ, we begin to see with eyes of faith what God is bringing forth, not by might, not by power, but by His Spirit. Man's hands "for" God won't produce the release of this harvest that is coming.

Christ has opened up for His church an enlarged place of the Spirit where we see past what we can see in the natural to what He is doing in the unseen realm. There is a generation of priests being raised up who are being trained to live from the unseen realm of the Spirit. God is calling hearts to live beyond what can be seen in the natural. "So we fix our eyes on what is unseen. For what is seen is temporary, but what is unseen is eternal" (2 Corinthians 4:18).

Christ has opened up for His church an enlarged place of the Spirit where nations can be impacted in the place of prayer. The place of prayer, God's way, is where His Spirit moves and works.

Barrenness filled with joy and a promise of enlargement produces descendants who dispossess nations. There is a generation of priests arising, crying out for revival and the awakening of a harvest of souls. There is a work in prayer that is filled with joy as we join with God's heart and the power of His Spirit to accomplish His plans and purposes, according to His ways.

From the place of this barrenness is released a faith that with Christ, all things become possible. There is a royal priesthood arising whose spiritual eyes are being opened to see the barren places all around them, the places empty of His life and presence, and are believing God to bring forth His life in those places. Whether it is the barrenness of others' lives and situations around them or their city, their own nation, or a foreign country, their hearts are being gripped by the Holy Spirit to believe, like Ezekiel, that the dry bones can live again. A royal priesthood is arising to establish altars of worship to the King of glory and are praying and prophesying that these barren places can come alive by His glory. "Lift up your heads, O you gates; be lifted up, you ancient doors, that the King of glory may come in" (Psalm 24:7). A hidden priesthood is crying out for the closed places to God's presence and His kingdom, to be opened up to more of His presence revealed and His spiritual kingdom demonstrated. There is no dark place God's light and presence can't penetrate and bring restoration to.

God gave my friend Sandee Mehojah this vision in Omaha on February 9, 2014. This is what she saw and sensed the Lord was saying during a time of corporate worship:

> The worship song had these words, "your presence, your presence is everything to me." As we repeated these words and worshiped, I saw this picture in panoramic view: I/we were standing in the sanctuary and/or on the land—gates that have been closed to us before were flung open as we worshiped Him. This happens because and when we worship Him—His presence then inhabits this worship and His word is released for a specific location or people. The strong, dark places that were once closed become open to the Lord and word of the Lord. As we stand looking into these places that were firmly closed, gates are flung open and the once-dark places and strongholds are

filled with light, with His presence. As we see this, it becomes our invitation to begin to walk through the gates, declaring and proclaiming the word of the Lord. The declarations must be what His gives us and not our words or our desires (as good as they may be). We must have ears to hear and eyes to see. The declaration was, "Our God reigns. Our God reigns. Everything must bow at the name of Jesus. His light is released into the darkness/the dark places. The peoples are released from captivity into His marvelous light! Our God reigns, our God reigns!" I believe the Lord is giving us an invitation during this season to move into the place of deeper and more intimate worship and begin to declare His words to the nations before people go and as they go into these areas. As we worship, the teams that go will become more effective.

This vision was specifically related to the reservations, specifically Nebraska, South Dakota, Montana and villages of Alaska, but this vision paints the picture of what gets opened up in the spiritual realm through worship. There are dark places everywhere. We live in dark times. I am not only talking about people going as missionaries to foreign countries. God is gripping hearts with the barrenness of man's efforts to pierce the darkness in the areas of education, business, science, and technology where man is exalted and there is no light and life of Jesus Christ.

As we worship and pray, dark places are opened up to His light and presence. Second Corinthians 4:4 shares, "The god of this age has blinded the minds of unbelievers so they cannot see the light of the gospel of the glory of Christ." This verse reveals that there is a spiritual reality where minds are being deceived. They are veiled. We are in a spiritual battle. Through worship, prayer, and declaration, spiritual veils are being removed. This brings an ease in the laboring and increases the effectiveness as He sends people to go into these dark places to bring the good news of the gospel of the glory of God in the face of Christ.

God is raising up a royal priesthood who will arise and shine, going into the culture and into the nations. As people go to where He is sending them, He gives hidden wisdom for His love and light to be released into those places. There are no formulas in this work of God. Man's formulas for building can't compare to God's wisdom and ways that reveal and release His love and life. These ways are readily available to anyone who will seek Him and be willing to surrender to His higher ways.

This priesthood that is rising up is being gripped with a vision of what God desires to do in the power of His Spirit. They are expecting harvest and are preparing. Their hearts are being stirred with radical obedience to Him. Therefore, "Enlarge the place of your tent, stretch your tent curtains wide, do not hold back, lengthen your cords" (Isaiah 54:2). The barren place of the cross of Christ is the entry point for fullness of life, freedom, and resurrection power. The cross of Christ is still the only entry point for the opening up of hearts and even whole regions to the power of Christ's love and His kingdom being revealed. The barren place of the cross of Jesus Christ is opening up an enlarged place of the Spirit's work, for Christ to be revealed in His fullness.

A Hidden Priesthood Revealing Christ

Strengthen your stakes. (Isaiah 54:2)

God is raising up a Melchizedek priesthood standing in the power of Jesus Christ's indestructible life because they have been anchored or staked to the love of Christ being released through the cross of Jesus Christ. A royal priesthood is arising, strengthening her stakes in the cross of Jesus Christ, unashamedly anchored there. Jesus words, in His call to follow Him in Luke 14:25, still ring true today: "If anyone comes to Me and does not hate father and mother, his wife and children, his brothers and sisters—yes, even his own life- he cannot be My disciple."

Every time we choose following Jesus in discipleship, His life springs forth from the barren place of "death to self."

The places that look barren with the natural eyes and impossible to penetrate, staked to the cross of Jesus Christ through our obedience to pick up our cross and follow Him, become places of springs from which others may drink deeply of Him. He calls us to embrace His life and go low in serving others.

> Your attitude should be the same as that of Christ: who being the very nature God, did not consider equality with God something to be grasped, but made himself nothing, taking the very nature of a servant ... he humbled himself and became obedient to death. (Philippians 2:5–8)

We are in an empowering season that Christ speaks of in John 6. The church will not just receive His benefits but receive His life. Following the same progression of John 6, we are moving through the courts of receiving supernatural provision, miracles, and healings, and come to His invitation to drink His flesh and eat His blood. We will be as the disciples when they declared they would not turn back as Jesus opened up the hard truth to them of what they were to walk in. "Lord, to whom shall we go? You have the words of eternal life." This is true freedom.

We will be a generation of priests who eat His flesh and drink His blood, being joined to Him in deeper ways, "for you will spread out to the right and left" (Isaiah 52:3).

We will drink His blood by opening our hearts fully to allow the blood of Christ to cleanse and cover us through and through.

> How much more, then, will the blood of Christ, who through the eternal Spirit offered himself unblemished to God, cleanse our consciences from acts that lead to death, so that we may serve the living God! (Hebrews 9:14)

Christ's perfect sacrifice of His shed blood does not just produce an outward washing that provides only a superficial cleaning. The blood of Jesus applied and "alive" in our hearts, cleans us thoroughly and deeply, setting us apart for His holy purposes. His blood washed us and changes us. There is life in His blood applied to our lives.

With the power of His blood alive in hearts, there is a generation of priests declaring in prayer over situations that the power of His blood is able to reconcile all things back to God.

> For God was pleased to have all his fullness dwell in him and through him to reconcile to himself all things, whether things on earth or things in heaven, by making peace through his blood, shed on the cross. (Colossians 1:19–20)

We will eat His flesh by doing His will as the Holy Spirit reveals and empowers. Not our will, but Your will be done, Father, following our beautiful Savior wherever He leads, turning the barren places into lush gardens as we worship the king of Glory. Seeing the glory of God revealed as His goodness is demonstrated. In John 14:18, Jesus assures us He would not leave us as orphans to do it on our own but will give us another like Him, the Holy Spirit, to lead us into all truth. We are no longer orphans. We are now sons through Jesus Christ. Only an heir will inherit the promises that are yes in Christ. Only a son will lay down His life for the will of His father. We have not been left on our own to offer the sacrifices we think we should offer, but we have been given the Holy Spirit to lead us into the will of the Father. Our own good sacrifices will not release the glory.

> On that day you will realize that I am in my Father, and you are in me, and I am in you. Whoever has my commands and obeys them, he is the one who loves me. He who loves me will be loved by my Father, and I too will love him and show myself to him. (John 14:20–21)

Not only is the Holy Spirit revealing the will of the Father, but He is also empowering our hearts in the offering. It is no longer about offering what we can do in our own strength and wisdom. We are discovering Him, and we are discovering His will and ways. We are with Him in the obeying, and there is joy just to be with Him, in whatever He is doing. We are eating His flesh as we enter into obeying His will out of love and devotion.

Paul's desire in Philippians is becoming the prayer of this royal priesthood that is arising. "I want to know Christ and the power of his resurrection and the fellowship of sharing in his sufferings, becoming like him in his death" (Philippians 3:7–10).

A royal priesthood is arising joined to Christ, not only in the power of His resurrection but also in the embracing of the fellowship of sharing in His sufferings that they might know Him more. To enter into fullness of knowing Christ, they must embrace both His power and His suffering. Christ is with them as they experience both. Even the suffering that comes through persecutions, false accusations, and misunderstandings, we are there with Him in it, fellowshipping with Him. He really does set a table before us in the presence of our enemies. Paul in Galatians 4:28 refers to what is born by the Spirit will be persecuted by the son "born the natural way." It speaks to the opposition that will come to those living by the Spirit. We are hidden in Him as we die to self and the need we have to be understood as we walk out His will and His ways. We learn to live for His approval alone, as He deals with the concern we have with how others view us.

We demonstrate our love for Him through obedience. This is a valuable key to walking in Christ's authority. We willingly and freely surrender to Christ's authority in our own lives, having His will worked into our lives, as we obey His word and love not our own lives. We find Him there, and we find true freedom in Him. Paul's message in Galatians fills our hearts with promise and encouragement to stand strong and live free in Christ.

> Get rid of the slave woman and her son, for the slave woman's son will never share in the inheritance with the free woman's son. Therefore, we are not children of the slave woman, but of the free woman. (Galatians 4:30)

We are a people born of the Spirit, living by the Spirit, laboring until Christ is formed in others.

> Your descendants will dispossess nations and settle in their desolate cities. (Isaiah 54:3)

A royal priesthood is arising, alive in Christ, joined to Christ, His life revealed in their mortal bodies. This is the key to spiritual warfare that the enemy cannot stand against. Paul spoke of a spiritual battle we find ourselves engaged in as priests of the Lord called into the darkness to release His marvelous light. It is not a worldly battle with earthly weapons. It is a spiritual battle with heaven's weapons of love and truth.

> For though we live in the world, we do not wage war as the world does. The weapons we fight with are not the weapons of the world. On the contrary, they have divine power to demolish strongholds. We demolish arguments and every pretension that sets itself up against the knowledge of God, and we take captive every thought to make it obedient to Christ. And we will be ready to punish every act of disobedience, once your obedience is complete. (2 Corinthians 10:4–6)

This is the simplicity of God's strategy for spiritual warfare: obedience to Christ. As we allow Christ's authority to reign in our hearts and minds, we can then release His authority that demolishes strongholds. Sometimes the greatest battle is simply in our own minds, as our natural thinking tries to oppose the ways of the Spirit, which can seem so foolish or contrary to everything we have ever been taught living in this culture. As we take every thought captive and bring it into obedience to Christ, freedom comes and His authority in prayer is given. The life of the Spirit is bringing forth a harvest. A kingdom of priests dispossesses the enemy by their surrender to Christ. Spiritual fruit from the place of intimacy in prayer dispossesses nations, stretching out to the left and to the right. "He is the vine, we are the branches" (John 15:5). All life flows from Him. "If a man remains in me and I in him, he *will* bear much fruit" (John 15:5).

A royal priesthood is arising, hidden in Christ, revealing Christ. His intent continues to be that:

> Now, through the church, the manifold wisdom of God should be made known to the rulers and authorities in the heavenly realms, according to his eternal purpose which he accomplished in Christ Jesus our Lord. In Him and through faith in him we may approach God with freedom and confidence. (Ephesians 3:10)

A royal priesthood is willing to wait on God and not build golden calves of their own making as a substitution for what God is bringing forth, not by might or power, but by His Spirit.

A royal priesthood is humbling themselves before God's perfect plan and surrendering to His way, the walk of faith.

A royal priesthood is willing to undergo intense preparation of the Spirit to bring their own hearts into obedience to God's will and His ways. They will undergo the seven days of preparation at the tent of meeting to receive God's ordination and anointing on the eighth day (Leviticus 8–9).

> I have been crucified with Christ and I no longer live, but Christ lives in me. The life I live in the body, I live by faith in the Son of God, who loved me and gave himself for me. (Galatians 2:20)

We declare that there is a generation of priests being joined to Christ, hidden in Him, freed in His love. Hearts are being released from other constraints and pursuits, free to love Him, free to live abandoned to Him. Hearts are becoming fully satisfied in God, running deeper into obedience to His will. We speak release in Jesus's name, to cords that still bind us and keep us from being bound to You, Jesus. Hearts are being stretched out to the right and left in obedience to Your will. We love You, Jesus. We love Your will, Father. You are the desire of our hearts, and we yield to Your ways.

5

Pure Offerings

My name will be great among the nations, from the rising
to the setting of the sun. In every place incense and pure
offerings will be brought to my name, because my name
will be great among the nations, says the Lord Almighty.

Malachi 1:11

In these verses, the Lord through Malachi is declaring a day when
God's name will be great among the nations and because of this,
pure offerings and incense will be offered.

In our time, God is stirring hearts with a cry for God's name to be
great among the nations and for pure offerings and incense that honor
God and bless His heart to be given. The prayer of, "God bless me"
has given way to a cry, "God, be great among the nations."

Just before Malachi makes this declaration, he begins to reveal in
1:6–7 that God has grown weary of their blemished sacrifices. It leads
God to declare, "Oh, that one of you would shut the temple doors, so
that you would not light useless fires on my altar!"

Valuable Fire

The old covenant priests were the ones who had the responsibility to keep the fires tended so they didn't go out. In Leviticus 6:12, God gives this command: "The fire on the altar must be kept burning; it must not go out … the fire must be kept burning on the altar continuously; it must not go out."

What had brought God to the point of saying He just wanted them to stop lighting fires on the altar so sacrifices couldn't be given? The fire on the altar is what burned the sacrifices and incense. In the book of Malachi, the prophet speaks to Israel about the condition of their sacrifices. The quality of the sacrifices had brought God to the point of saying He wanted to shut the temple doors. These verses speak to the issue of the priests offering blemished sacrifices. The best was not being given. Even though sacrifices where still being offered, they were not the sacrifices God was asking for. It was only in duty because God's name was no longer great in their hearts. The fires had become useless. God knew the condition of where their hearts had strayed.

In Malachi 3:1, He promises to come, "As a refiner's fire to purify the Levites and refine them like gold so that the Lord will have men who bring offerings in righteousness, and the offerings will be acceptable again."

This refiner's fire that will refine the Levites so that offerings are restored to purity. God's fire tests the offerings. We can invite the fire now to test the quality of the offerings of our lives. All will be tested by the fire.

> But each should be careful how he builds. For no one can lay any foundation other than the one already laid, which is Jesus Christ. If any man builds on this foundation using gold, silver, costly stones, wood, hay or straw, his work will be shown for what it is, because the Day will bring it to light. It will be revealed with fire, and the fire will test the quality of each man's work. (1 Corinthians 3:11–13)

What is the fire that God values, that He doesn't deem as useless? To keep the fires from becoming useless as God declared in Malachi is for them to be a refiner's fire that restores pure devotion to Christ.

A royal priesthood is arising, continually tending the fires of devotion to Christ in their hearts. A royal priesthood is arising, calling Christ's church, His bride, to sincere and pure devotion to Christ.

Paul wrote to the church in Corinth, beckoning them to return:

> I hope you will put up with a little of my foolishness; but you are already doing that. I am jealous for you with a godly jealousy. I promised you to one husband, to Christ, so that I might present you as a pure virgin to him. But I am afraid that just as Eve was deceived by the serpent's cunning, your minds may somehow be led astray from your sincere and pure devotion to Christ. For if someone comes to you and preaches a Jesus other than the Jesus we preached, or if you receive a different spirit from the one you received, or a different gospel from the one you accepted, you put up with it easily enough. (2 Corinthians 11:1–4)

The dictionary definition of the word *sincere* is "free from pretense; wholehearted." The word *sincere* stresses the absence of any hypocrisy or any falsifying embellishment or exaggeration. Wholehearted suggests sincerity and earnest devotion without reservation.

The word *pure* is defined as "not mixed with any other substance; free from anything of a different or inferior nature."

The word *devotion* means "loyalty, faithfulness, profound dedication. State of being ardently (fiery hot, zealous), speaks of passion."

Paul's heart, because it burned with devotion to Christ, was jealous that Christ alone receive the wholehearted devotion of His bride.

In the above passages, Paul uses the words *deception* and *led astray*.

"Led astray" implies a gradual movement away from the mark or center. It can happen over time, without any awareness that we are going in the wrong direction because it is so gradual.

We think of deception as something that happens to those not in the church. Paul is speaking to the church, and he refers to how Eve was deceived by Satan. Satan offered her something that appeared good, that would make her "wise."

In these verses, Paul speaks of things that he was concerned would lead their minds astray from the anchor of sincere and pure devotion to Christ: "A Jesus other than the one we preached." "A different spirit from the one you received." "A different gospel from the one you accepted, you put up with it easily enough."

It was still Jesus being preached, not Mohammad, not Buddha, etc. It was a different Jesus. In the modern-day American church, it is still Jesus being preached, but He no longer requires death to self. He only wants us to be "happy" or "rich." Suffering has been removed from the equation. Sin no longer is spoken of. The moving of the Spirit will just turn people off. There isn't room in our services. We have to ask the question, have we stopped making room for the Holy Spirit's work in our individual lives? Mary, the mother of Jesus, made room for the Holy Spirit's work in her life, and it brought reproach to her name and disrupted everything in her life. Is it a different spirit we have received?

In our world of technology and expanding knowledge and human wisdom, have our churches easily accepted another gospel so we could fit in and be "accepted" by the world so we could "win" them to Jesus? Have we eaten the apple of deception? Is it a different gospel not centered around sincere and pure devotion to Christ? Have we put up with this as easily as the Corinthians did? Has it so gradually become mixed with the wisdom of this age that we weren't even aware that our devotion was losing its purity and sincerity?

The gospel Paul embraced required him to become simple and "foolish." In 1 Corinthians, he speaks of God confusing the human wisdom of the age with godly "foolishness."

> For the message of the cross is foolishness to those who are perishing, but to us who are being saved it is the power of God. For it is written: "I will destroy the

wisdom of the wise; the intelligence of the intelligent I will frustrate." Where is the wise man? Where is the scholar? Where is the philosopher of this age? Has not God made foolish the wisdom of the world? ... For the foolishness of God is wiser than man's wisdom, and the weakness of God is stronger than man's strength. (1 Corinthians 1:18–25)

Paul was wise and learned by human standards. He chose to empty himself of those accomplishments to receive God's wisdom and strength.

When I came to you, brothers, I did not come with eloquence or superior wisdom as I proclaimed to you the testimony about God. For I resolved to know nothing while I was with you except Jesus Christ and him crucified. I came to you in weakness and fear, and with much trembling. My message and my preaching were not with wise and persuasive words, but with a demonstration of the Spirit's power, so that your faith might not rest on men's wisdom, but on God's power. (1 Corinthians 2:1–4)

Paul chose not to let himself rest and trust in his wise and persuasive words of knowledge about the scriptures but trusted in the demonstration of the Spirit's power as he came in weakness, so that the Corinthians' faith would not be in the knowledge of scriptures but in the power of God. Paul firmly believed that the "foolishness" of God's way was wiser than man's wisdom and could be trusted. He refused to mix the gospel with man's wisdom. His priestly calling to minister to Christ kept him burning with devotion and the desire to see a pure offering given to God.

Because of the grace of God gave me to be a minister of Christ Jesus to the Gentiles with the priestly duty of proclaiming the gospel of God, so that the Gentiles might become an offering acceptable to God, sanctified by the Holy Spirit. (Romans 15:16)

In the New King James Version, 2 Corinthians 11:3 reads in this way: "But I fear, lest somehow, as the serpent deceived Eve by his craftiness, so your minds may be corrupted from the simplicity that is in Christ."

A computer drive, when it becomes corrupted, must be wiped clean. It must have its defaults reset. If our minds are corrupted from this place of simplicity of devotion to Christ, the Holy Spirit's work must reset our settings.

> Those who live in accordance with the Spirit have their *minds set* on what the Spirit desires. (Romans 8:5)

What "drives" us? What consumes us? What are we desiring? This speaks of passions, a definition of the word *devotion*. This is about truth in our innermost parts: all of us, in our deepest thoughts and intentions of our hearts, where no one else sees, turned to God, loving Him, ministering to Him, not holding anything back from Him, placing Him as the source of our trust in all things.

I have a degree in accounting and have worked in finance in both business and churches. I have observed people's attitude toward money in various settings. Over the last twenty years, the Holy Spirit has at different times revealed to my heart mind-sets I have had toward money that I wasn't even aware of. I have become more keenly aware of Jesus's words that we can't love money and Him. Could the word *love* also be substituted with the word *depend* without changing its meaning? What I mean by this is, is there a dependency on money that has become a substitute for our dependency on God? We can't depend on money and on Him. Which are we depending on and trusting in—God or money? We live in a culture where money is a false god. Is money driving our decisions, even in the church? We have to consider this question.

For us to be free in His love to go where He sends us and do what He asks us, we must be freed of these constraints of the culture of our society and even the cultures of the world, that are operating in the church. The power that money holds in our culture must be broken in our lives so the power of the Spirit can be activated in a greater measure and a greater dimension of the provision of His kingdom can be released. We are called to depend on and be led by His Spirit. A royal priesthood is arising whose pursuit is His unshakeable kingdom. This is what they are learning to trust in.

This returns us to where we started in Malachi. There is a promise of God given in Malachi 3:1–4:

> "See, I will send my messenger, who will prepare the way before me. Then suddenly the Lord you are seeking will come to his temple; the messenger of the covenant, whom you desire, will come," says the Lord Almighty. But who can endure the day of his coming? Who can stand when he appears; For he will be like a refiner's fire or a launderer's soap. He will sit as a refiner and purifier of silver. He will purify the Levites and refine them like gold and silver. Then the Lord will have men who will bring offerings in righteousness, and the offerings of Judah and Jerusalem will be acceptable to the Lord, as in days gone by, as in former years ago.

God invites us to welcome His refiner's fire on the sacrifice of our lives, to test our hearts and restore the purity to the offerings and incense. We will talk more later about God's fire, but for now we need to understand God's fire is not like natural fire that is destructive. The reality that there is a future fire that will eternally burn for those who have ultimately rejected Him has left some fearful of His fire. We can trust His fire of love upon our hearts. His intentions toward us are always good, to give us a hope and a future. He longs to remove those things from our lives that are keeping us from depending on Him and trusting Him. He has promised to baptize us with the Holy Spirit and fire, to restore pure, simple devotion to Him.

Pure Offerings and Incense

In the tabernacle of Moses in the Old Testament, there were two types of altars and a lampstand. There was the brazen altar or altar of sacrifice and the altar of incense. There was a lampstand that burned pure oil.

A royal priesthood is arising who in their lives have built these altars and lampstand. Because His name is great in their hearts, they long to see these pure offerings and incense given. The first place these are established is in their own hearts.

An Altar of Sacrifice

Jesus, full of light and the glory of heaven, clothed himself in earth's humanity. The book of Genesis tells us that man started out as the dirt of the earth. We are told in Genesis 2:7, "The Lord God formed the man from the dust of the ground." For an offering to be made, there was always a place where the sacrifice was given: an altar. In Exodus 20:24, God commanded Moses and the Israelites to build an altar of earth.

> You shall make an altar of earth for me, and you will sacrifice on it your burnt offerings and your peace offerings, your sheep and your oxen; Wherever I cause my name to be honored, I will come to you and bless you.

God's name is honored everywhere an altar is built. Jesus built the altar of earth by becoming a man. Jesus's heart was to honor His Father. There is a promise of blessing that is attached to this building of an altar. Jesus's life became the altar to honor His Father and to release the blessing of the glory of heaven upon all humankind.

The altar of sacrifice is where the burnt offerings for sin were made in the Old Testament. In the Old Testament, God was very specific about the kind of offering that could be offered on the altar that would be acceptable to Him. The burnt offering was a voluntary, willing sacrifice. It represented the highest form of offering. It was given in an effort to renew the relationship between holy God and man.

We see Jesus, from the altar of His life, releasing the perfect sacrifice, a willing offering, pleasing and acceptable to His Father. Jesus honored His Father by voluntarily submitting to His will. Hebrews 10:5 shares Jesus's words regarding His Father's desire:

> Sacrifice and offering you did not desire, but a body you

prepared for me; With burnt offerings and sin offerings you were not pleased. Then I said, "Here I am—it is written about me in the scroll—I have come to do your will, O God.

Jesus's perfect sacrifice completed the work of restoration to renew the relationship between God and man. No other sacrifice is needed. Jesus is the only perfect, sinless sacrifice. In this hour, God is liberating hearts from serving Him in duty, and they are being given over to delight. Their hearts resound with the song of David, "I delight to do your will O My God." A royal priesthood is arising with pure offerings of devotion to Christ. They are building altars of earth in their own hearts. From out of weak, earthen vessels, they are offering themselves to God as living sacrifices, holy and pleasing to God. It is a spiritual worship. They are offering Christ's perfect sacrifice as they join themselves to God and His ways, and it is causing the glory of God to be released over others' lives.

I urge you brothers, in view of God's mercy, to offer your bodies as living sacrifices, holy and pleasing to God, this is your spiritual act of worship. (Romans 12:1)

Out of the revelation of God's mercy to us, we offer ourselves to God. There is no drudgery in this offering. There is pure joy in the offering, as we are going with Him, encountering His living presence along the way. A royal priesthood is arising that desires to be with Him wherever He is going.

Abraham responded when God called him to offer his own son, the son of promise. Without this son, how could God's promise be fulfilled, Abraham might have wondered? Abraham had faith in his heart for the perfect sacrifice to fulfill what God was asking. This reality produced a heart willing to offer whatever God asked for. Abraham honored God and obeyed God. Abraham had faith and trust in God.

In Genesis 22:8–14, Abraham says to his son,

God himself will provide the lamb for the burnt offering, my son. When they reached the place God told him about, Abraham built an altar there and arranged the wood. Abraham looked up and there in a thicket he saw a ram caught by its horns. He went over and took the ram and sacrificed it as a burnt offering instead of his son. So Abraham called that place the Lord will Provide.

Everything God asks us to do, He has gone ahead to provide everything that is needed to fulfill what He is asking of us.

There is a Melchizedek priesthood arising, being joined to Christ's indestructible life and His kingly authority. They are honoring God by building altars of sacrifice in their own lives. From these altars, they are offering pure and simple devotion to Christ. This is releasing the blessing of the glory of heaven to others.

Lampstand Full of Oil

A royal priesthood is arising who has a lampstand full of oil. Jesus described John in this way: "John was a lamp that burned and gave light, and you chose for a time to enjoy his light" (John 5:35).

Zechariah's vision shows a golden lampstand with pure oil that empowers God's works:

> I see a solid gold lampstand with a bowl at the top and seven lights on it, with seven channels to the lights. Also there are two olive trees by it, one on the right of the bowl and the other on its left. I asked the angel who talked with me, "What are these, my lord?" "Do you not know these are?" "No, my lord," I replied. So he said to me, "This is the word of the Lord to Zerubbabel; 'Not by might nor by power, but by my Spirit,' says the Lord Almighty." (Zechariah 4:1–6)

The Holy Spirit is this pure oil we are to be continually filled with. He is what fuels the fire of devotion to Christ upon our hearts. The Holy Spirit empowers hearts with hunger and purifies offerings and incense. This will require fellowship with the Holy Spirit. It will take time to learn to listen to His voice. It will require us making room for His filling.

Jesus tells the parable of the five wise virgins and the five foolish virgins.

> At that time the kingdom of heaven will be like ten virgins who took their lamps and went out to meet the bridegroom. Five of them were foolish and five were wise. The foolish ones took their lamps but did not take any oil with them. The wise, however, took oil in jars along with their lamps. (Matthew 25:1–5)

The wise virgins had oil for their lamps when the bridegroom came. A royal priesthood is filled with the oil of His Spirit. This priesthood is tending the lampstand continually through cultivating time spent fellowshipping with the Holy Spirit.

In Leviticus 24:2–4, God commanded Aaron to tend the lamps:

> Command the Israelites to bring you clear oil of pressed olives for the light so that the lamps may be kept burning continually. Outside the curtain of the Testimony in the Tent of Meeting, Aaron is to tend the lamps before the Lord from evening till morning, continually. This is to be a lasting ordinance for the generations to come. The lamps on the pure gold lampstand before the Lord must be tended continually.

The New Testament counterpart to these verses is Paul's instructions in the book of Ephesians to be wise and not foolish.

> Therefore, do not be foolish, but understand what the Lord's will is. Do not get drunk on wine, which leads to sin. Instead, be filled with the Spirit. (Ephesians 5:17–18)

An Altar of Incense

In the hearts of this royal priesthood, there is the altar of sacrifice and the lampstand full of oil. The fires are kept continually burning. There is also an altar of incense.

The Old Testament (OT) priesthood was commanded by the Lord in Exodus 30:7 to regularly burn incense on the altar:

Aaron must burn fragrant incense on the altar every morning when he tends the lamps. He must burn incense again when he lights the lamps at twilight so incense will burn regularly before the Lord for the generations to come.

In Psalm 141:2, David describes this incense: "May my prayer be set before you like incense; may the lifting up of my hands be like the evening sacrifice."

The incense represents our prayers, praise, worship, and intercessions. This royal priesthood that is arising will be found releasing a regular and continual burning of incense from the fire of devotion to Christ that is kept burning on their hearts.

> He came and took the scroll from the right hand of him who sat on the throne. And when he had taken it, the four living creatures and the twenty-four elders fell down before the Lamb. Each one had a harp and they were holding golden bowls full of incense, which are the prayers of the saints. And they sang a new song. (Revelation 5:8)

John's revelation of the throne room shows that the offering of incense on earth is joining with heaven's worship. Our prayers are kept in golden bowls. It doesn't matter how small and weak these prayers seem in the natural; they are beautiful to the Lord. He holds them. These prayers matter to Him. They touch and move His heart.

A royal priesthood is arising, coming before Him in worship, prayer, and intercessions. The word *intercede* simply means a prayer on behalf of someone else. Romans 8:34 says that Jesus is presently sitting at the right hand of the Father interceding for us. A royal priesthood joined to Jesus's heart, joined to His intercessions, standing in Him in the place of intercession. It is not just a select group of people called intercessors. From His finished work, Jesus's present work is that of interceding for us (Romans 8:34). If "He ever lives to make intercession" and "we no longer live but Christ lives in us" (Galatians 2:20), then the High Priest and Apostle of our faith lives in every born-again believer and we are *all* called to intercession, not just a select group of people,

As we sit with Jesus in worship, prayer, and intercessions, we come just to be with Him. We leave agendas aside and allow the oil of the Holy Spirit to fill our praying. We invite His plans to invade our planning. We give Him our burdens, and we take His yoke.

> In the same way, the Spirit helps us in our weakness. We do not know what we ought to pray for, but the Spirit himself intercedes for us. And he who searches our heart, knows the mind of the Spirit, because the Spirit intercedes for the saints in accordance with God's will. (Romans 8:26)

The Holy Spirit's work in our hearts giving to us the fullness of God's heart and will. First Corinthians 2:9–12 puts it this way:

> "No eye has seen no ear has heard no mind has conceived what God has prepared for those who love him—but God has revealed it to us by His Spirit." The Spirit searches all things, even the deep things of God. For who among men know the thoughts of a man except the man's spirit within him? In the same way no one knows the thoughts of God except the Spirit of God.

The Holy Spirit is present with us, leading us to agree with Jesus's perfect intercessions in our praying. Our hearts are stirred by His heart as we pray His word. Our prayers and intercessions are being purified. Christ's living body in the earth is standing in the place of intercession. His decrees and declarations are being made on earth as they are in heaven.

Songs of worship are being sung and bowls of intercession are being filled up, and His purposes are being released upon the earth. This can happen anywhere, anytime, as the Holy Spirit leads. You can be driving in your car, declaring His words that He gives over situations that He places on your heart. You can be sitting in your office and draw into the secret place of your heart to worship Him. You can be doing dishes, ministering to Jesus, and listening to the still, small voice of the Holy Spirit.

As a mom, my heart is so blessed when I hear my kids begin to spontaneously sing songs of worship to Jesus as they are playing in their rooms or doing the dishes together. It touches my heart. I know it blesses God's heart as their worship is released. Their simple worship moves things in the spiritual realm.

In the gospel of Mark, there is the story of a woman bringing a "wasteful" offering to Jesus, a picture of sincere and pure devotion to Christ. It was an offering given purely in love and gratitude to Jesus, for no other purpose, but it served a holy purpose, to prepare Him for His burial. She was an extravagant worshiper, discerning the times and season of His death.

> Now the Passover and the Feast of Unleavened Bread were only two days away, and the chief priests and the teachers of the law were looking for some sly way to arrest Jesus and kill him. But not during the Feast, they said, "or the people may riot." While he was in Bethany, reclining at the table in the home of a man known as Simon the Leper, a woman came with an alabaster jar of very expensive perfume, made of pure nard. She broke the jar and poured the perfume on his head. Some of those present were saying indignantly to one another, "Why this waste of perfume? It could have been sold for more than a year's wages and the money given to the poor." And they rebuked her harshly. "Leave her alone," said Jesus. "Why are you bothering her? She has done a beautiful thing to me. The poor you will always have with you, and you can help them any time you want. But you will not always have me. She did what she could. She poured perfume on my body beforehand to prepare for my burial." (Mark 14:1–8)

It was an offering that would be remembered and retold wherever the gospel was preached. There was a simplicity of devotion that is powerful, unlocking the testimony of Jesus through pure, simple worship. "I tell you the truth, wherever the gospel is preached throughout the world, what she has done will also be told" (Mark 14:9). It was not given to accomplish this, but it did accomplish this. The woman's "wasting" of costly resources given in extravagant worship caused indignation among those present. Her act of pure worship also revealed the hearts of others in the room.

Holy Spirit, break open our hearts to release an offering of worship from our lives that is pure and wholly devoted to Christ. *All for you, Jesus.* There is a release of an aroma of His presence from our lives broken open. This is the point where our offerings become "wasteful," serving no "good" purpose other than to bless His heart, just pure extravagance of devotion poured out at Jesus's feet.

> "In every place incense and pure offerings will be brought to my name, because my name WILL be great among the nations," says the Lord Almighty. (Malachi 1:11)

6

Priests Carrying His Presence

The book of Joshua tells the story of the children of Israel crossing over into the land that had been promised to Abraham hundreds of years before. A journey into Egypt, and seventy family members going into Egypt, come out as a multitude four hundred years later. Through a lack of trust in God's ability to perform His word, they would wander in the wilderness, dying off there. Forty years later, their children would possess the promise.

A new day dawns. "After the death of Moses, the Lord said to Joshua, "Now then, you and all these people, get ready to cross the Jordan River I am giving you" (Joshua 1:1).

It is the season of fulfillment of promises long delayed. A new day is dawning on the life of the church as we are awakened to resurrection life and rise up to walk through the open door. We are in a new season of crossing over into fullness in Christ, being led by the Holy Spirit, dependent on the Spirit, empowered by the Spirit.

When the word came to cross, it would be the priests who would be the ones carrying the presence of God, to take the first step of obedience, stepping into the raging waters during flood stage. Who are those individuals God is raising up in this late hour in history to open up the flood waters to entrance into the promises of God through acts of obedience empowered by His love and grace?

> At that time the Lord set apart the tribe of Levi to carry the ark of the covenant of the Lord, to stand before the Lord to minister and to pronounce blessings in his name. That is why the Levites have no share or inheritance among their brothers; the Lord is their inheritance, as the Lord your God told them. (Deuteronomy 10:8–9)

There is a new covenant priesthood that is arising, being prepared as they are hidden in Christ, whose only inheritance they desire is fullness in Christ. Jesus is the land of promise. Jesus is the longing and desire of the hearts of this priesthood. Devotion to Christ will be the strength on their hearts to step out to follow Him wherever He would lead. Out of this devotion to Christ a rich faith and trust in God is being released to possess His promises.

> When you see the ark of the covenant of the Lord your God, and the priests, who are Levites, carrying it, you are to move out from your positions and follow it. Then you will know which way to go, since you have never been this way before. (Joshua 3:3)

A Gazing Priesthood

When you see the ark of the covenant of the Lord your God...

This new priesthood that is arising is being trained in the art of gazing. This priesthood has their eyes on Jesus. They are following the ark of His presence. They have embraced a disciplined lifestyle of setting their hearts continually before the Lord. A daily quiet time done in duty will not be enough for those whose hearts are set on a pilgrimage to know their God and be found in Him. It is not legalism to say that it will require an intentional disciplining of the heart to set aside time to enter into a "one-thing" life. This is a strengthening of the heart's muscle to be still and know that He is God. This is true freedom to turn away from gazing on lesser things to behold the one who really matters.

David's heart cry in Psalm 27:4 has become this priesthood's heart cry:

> One thing I ask of the Lord, this is what I seek; that I may dwell in the house of the Lord all the days of my life, to gaze upon the beauty of the Lord and to seek him.

This priesthood has heeded the words of their Savior to Mary in Luke 10:38–41. Though they are passionate about the harvest that is ready, they work from a position of resting at their Bridegroom's feet.

> "Martha, Martha," the Lord answered, "you are worried and upset about many things, but only *one thing* is needed."

This priesthood will endure the misunderstanding of others to stay at Jesus's feet, understanding that in this hour, only one thing is needed: to be found listening to His words. Joshua was instructed by God in Joshua 1:8 to "not let the book of the Law depart from your mouth; meditate on it day and night." There is a call of the Spirit to regularly and continually feed on His words; this is our bread.

Carrying His Presence

And the priests who are Levites, carrying it.

This new covenant priesthood that is arising is carrying His presence. In this present church culture, there has been a training to follow those who can draw the crowds the quickest, or have certain degrees or accomplishments, or those who say the right things, but the mark of this priesthood's leadership will be that they are found carrying the aroma of His presence.

The story is told about Charles Finney, who carried the presence of God so strongly in his life that a whole factory was shut down from working because of God's presence touching hearts when Charles Finney made a visit.

From the article "Charles G. Finney: Groundbreaking Revivalist" by Ken Horn: "Evangelist Charles Finney had been touring the facility. As Finney simply observed the machinery, one worker, then another sank to the floor and burst into tears."[1]

"The impression caught almost like powder," said Finney in his autobiography, "and in a few moments nearly all in the room were in tears."

Finney, not with eloquent words but through an encounter with the presence of Christ that was resting on Finney's life, brought a whole room of people to tears, and production in the factory was shut down to make room for God to have His way. God's presence on a life changed the spiritual atmosphere of a factory.

In Exodus 30:22, the Lord commanded Moses to use specific ingredients and specific measures to make the anointing oil that would be used to anoint the tent of meeting, all the articles, and Aaron and his sons as priests.

This new covenant priesthood is being anointed with the anointing of Christ. They are embracing God's prescribed way of allowing the light of His presence to penetrate the dark areas of their own hearts. His anointing that breaks every yoke going deep in them. They are not satisfied to look good on the outside but be found wanting on the inside.

The light of Christ shining on this new priesthood's hearts is their life. "In him was life, and that life was the light of men. The light shines in the darkness, but the darkness has not understood it" (John 1:3–5).

In Luke 4:14, it says of Jesus as He returned from the desert to Galilee in the power of the Spirit that He went to Nazareth and went into the synagogue. There He picked up the scroll of Isaiah and read the words:

> The Spirit of the Lord is on me, because he has anointed
> me to preach good news to the poor. He has sent me to

---

[1]Article called *Charles G. Finney: Groundbreaking Revivalist* by Ken Horn, from a series in the *Pentecostal Evangel* January 11, 2009.

proclaim freedom for the prisoners and recovery of sight for the blind, to release the oppressed, to proclaim the year of the Lord's favor.

The prophetic word of Isaiah was fulfilled through Christ, the anointed one. Christ's anointing is resting upon this priesthood who has come to rest in His presence. A holy, consecrated priesthood is arising in this time to carry Christ's anointing into the darkness, releasing His marvelous light.

A Change of Direction

Move out from your positions and follow it. Then you will know which way to go, since you have never been this way before.

There is a transitioning from the old to the new in these verses. There is a need to leave the old to enter into the new. He says to move out from your position. We are creatures of habit. We find comfort in the familiar. We get entrenched very quickly in patterns and mind-sets. Sometimes these mind-sets are born out of self-protection. We do this with scripture even, using it to fortify our ideas intended to make us feel safe in our position or understanding of who God is. Is this possibly an explanation for why there are so many different interpretations of scriptures that have led to breakoffs and divisions in Christ's body?

How do we use scripture to fortify ourselves in self-protection? When fear of the unknown is operating in our lives, it can work to keep us from being open to Christ's gifts operating through other parts of Christ's body. It can cause us to not be open to receiving all that Christ wants to release in our lives through those other parts of His living body. Ephesians 4:11 says,

It is Christ that gives some to be apostles, prophets, evangelists, and some to be pastors and teachers, to prepare God's people until we all reach unity in the faith, and in the knowledge of the Son of God and become mature, attaining to the whole measure of the fullness of Christ.

We receive Christ when we receive His gifts and callings through others. We won't receive all of Christ if we don't receive those He sends to help equip us. There is more that He is holding out to us. He is calling us to move out from mind-sets that would limit our receiving what He has for us through others in His body.

If I only stay among my own denomination or group of people operating in the same operation of giftings, or among people of the same culture, I will never receive all of the diversity of Christ that works among His whole body. He is causing us to become a kingdom of priests, from every tribe, tongue, and nation as *His* kingdom's culture begins to rule over every other kingdom's culture in our hearts.

> The body is a unit, though it is made up of many parts;
> and though all its parts are many, they form one body.
> So it is with Christ. (1 Corinthians 12:12)

About eighteen years ago, God began to enlarge my heart with His love and plan concerning Native people here in the United States. He began to bring me into relationship with those of this culture that I had not previously been connected with. God started this work in me by bringing Dobie and Jamie Weasel to Omaha to be the pastors of the church I was a part of. Prior to meeting Dobie and Jamie, I can't recall knowing personally anyone who was Native American.

During this period of time, I was also brought into a meeting with a Native woman named Sandra Mehojah. I had been asked by Dobie to attend a prayer gathering to do work in prayer concerning Native injustices. At this point in my life, I had a passion for God and the place of prayer but had very little understanding of what Native people had walked through.

Sandra is a member of the Kaw Nation of Oklahoma. Her grandparents are Jesse and Maggie Mehojah, and her father is William Mehojah, who was the last pureblood of the Kaw Nation, and she is of the Night Clan. Sandra grew up living on several reservations, including Northern Cheyenne (Lame Deer, Montana), Rosebud Sioux (Rosebud, South Dakota), Standing Rock Sioux (Fort Yates, North Dakota), Turtle Mountain Chippewa (Belcourt, North Dakota), and

Shoshone-Bannock in Fort Hall, Idaho. In her own words, "During those years I saw and experienced continued injustices and oppression of Native people. Our voices had been silenced, belittled, and ignored for generations as well as in the present day."

Sandra describes the day of the prayer gathering in this way:

> It was an exciting time for me to be asked to be a part of this prayer work. I was new to intercession and new to how it all could work to address issues concerning people, the land, and the nations. I was also new to how intercession could work to address assignments given by God to specific hidden groups. I was in awe as I saw Native people who lived in another city and state come to intercede on behalf of people in another city, state, and nation. I felt this was a time of learning and watching how intercession operated and worked among people who had just met one another and had never really had any type of relationship with one another— but who had come together for a specific prayer assignment. Needless to say, I was in awe of the whole day and thankful that I was given this opportunity.
>
> It was at this time I met Debbie Goodwater. Her pastor had asked that she participate in this prayer work and travel with us as we went about the city. We ended up going to a specific place in the city that was important to Native people as this was the campus where the Trial of Chief Standing Bear, Ponca, was held and all it represented to Native people. We met in a grassy garden dedicated to Native people and to the memory of this trial.

On this day, during the time on the campus in the prayer garden, as we began to pray, God began to speak to my heart a word that He wanted me to share. He told me to ask Sandee, "Will you receive on behalf of Native people the love of God through whatever vessel He chooses to release it through?" At that point in my life, it was a huge step for me to step out and share in front of a group of people I did not know, what I sensed the Lord was speaking to me. With great hesitation, not wanting to be out of order with what God was doing, but in that moment, I was experiencing the love of God for Native people in such a profound way that I was compelled to ask the question God was putting in my heart to ask specifically to Sandee. I was not prepared for Sandee's answer.

Sandee shares her experience of this time,

> It was during this time, as we were praying, that out of the blue, Debbie specifically asked me if I would accept the love of God through white people. That question assaulted my whole being. I was totally flabbergasted at the question and also by the one who was asking the question. I wondered within myself, *Who is this white woman I have never met before asking me such a thing? Why do they always have to want to seemingly come in and take over and be a leading part in everything? Doesn't she understand what has happened to us in the past by the so-called missionaries' workings and dealings through their denominations? Why can't we just be allowed to determine our own path and how we (as Native people) will present the gospel on Indian lands and to Native people?*
>
> I just wanted to be left alone by her and the people she represented! And how dare she ask such a question in front of all these people? To me, it definitely seemed out of order and not in the flow with what was happening that day.
>
> What wasn't out of order or out of the flow that day was God's purposes for me and Debbie and what our relationship would represent in intercession. What wasn't out of order was what God was bringing to the forefront on that day by showing me I needed to deal

with the issues of my heart on behalf of myself and other native people. How was I going to deal with working alongside of white people for the spreading of the gospel and the prayer assignments of the Lord?

I left the meeting that day feeling embarrassed that I had stepped out and shared, not understanding at all what had gone on. In addition to my own emotions I was battling, I continued to experience an intense love of God for Native people for the rest of that day.

That day, strangely enough, would be the beginning of a friendship and partnership in prayer between Sandee and me that spans many years now. God would stir both of our hearts after that day to move out past our own feelings and trust Him that He had a plan in bringing us together.

My life and walk with the Lord is richer and deeper because of my friendship with Sandee. God has used us in each other's lives as iron sharpening iron. At times we have had to press past mind-sets that would try to divide us. We have discovered that the differences of our cultures can't divide us because the cross and blood of Jesus unites us. This bond is stronger, and every other allegiance must bend its knee to the lordship of Jesus Christ in our lives.

Mind-Sets Developed When God Moved in the Past

As we move out of past positions to follow Christ in this new day that is dawning on the life of His church, there are also mind-sets and patterns we have developed from how God moved in the past in our lives. These ways in which we have walked are how He called us to walk in a past season but may not have His life on it moving into the future. It is time to live beyond our histories, whatever they have been, and move into the future that God is opening up. We must stay connected to the Holy Spirit in this process. This is what was happening as John's disciples came to Jesus. Matthew 9:14–17 gives us their question and Jesus's response.

> Then John's disciples came and asked him, "How is it that we and the Pharisees fast, but your disciples do not

fast?" Jesus answered, "How can the guests of the bridegroom mourn while he is with them; The time will come when the bridegroom will be taken from them; then they will fast. No one sews a patch of unshrunk cloth on an old garment, for the patch will pull away from the garment, making the tear worse. Neither do men pour new wine into old wineskins. If they do, the skins will burst, the wine will run out and the wineskins will be ruined. No, they pour new wine into new wineskins, and both are preserved."

The new wineskin is what will hold the new wine God is releasing. We serve a God who is unchangeable, the same yesterday, today, and forever. The truth of His words found in the Bible must be the foundation of our lives. Our lives must be built on the rock, Christ Jesus. He doesn't change.

Jesus's words describe the changing work of the Holy Spirit as the wind, breathing upon the written word. Jesus's words to His disciples in John 14:16 were that in His going He would send another one who was "to be with you forever—the Spirit of truth" to lead us into all truth." The words *to lead* indicate movement. His truth isn't changing. It is our understanding of His truth that is.

In John 3:5 Jesus told Nicodemus, a religious leader of the day, when he came to Jesus inquiring how to be born again:

> I tell you the truth, no one can enter the kingdom of God unless he is born of water and the Spirit. Flesh gives birth to flesh, but the Spirit gives birth to spirit. You should not be surprised at my saying, "You must be born again. The wind blows wherever it pleases. You hear its sound, but you cannot tell where it comes from or where it is going. So it is with everyone born of the Spirit."

We must have the Spirit of truth, the Holy Spirit, active in our hearts, blowing upon the word, to know what God is saying. The sons of God will be led by the Spirit of God.

Peter, full of the Holy Spirit, had the wind of the Spirit blow upon His revelation of God's word, and it shook him into a new position of understanding, forming a new wineskin. The gospel was being opened up to the Gentiles, and God asked Peter to do what was previously forbidden by the law of God. The account of what happened can be found in Acts 10. The doors were being opened to all people to receive the glorious light of the gospel of Jesus Christ. Though the Jewish people would remain God's special beloved people, it was time for the nations to be grafted in. "But now in Christ Jesus you who once were far away have been brought near through the blood of Christ" (Ephesians 2:13).

"Keep Moving"

God began to release a fresh wind on the book of Joshua several years ago to our church body in Seward. We had served the Lord there for eight years. As His word was released, God began to speak personally to us as well from the above verses in Joshua 3:3. He said it was time to move out from our present position of serving as pastors. He was calling us to get up and move from our physical location. We did not know where we were going. My heart felt like it was being ripped out because I loved God's work there and I loved the people.

As we crossed over in faith into the new season God was opening up, I began to realize how much my heart longs to stay in what I know and understand. There is security that is found in the familiar. When God begins to move forward into a new way of working or manifesting His life to us, we must get up and move in our hearts and minds to a new place of seeing and understanding His ways, or our hearts may begin to darken and grow cold if we stay where we are in our mind-sets as He moves to lead us forward.

The depths of the revelation of Christ are limitless. This means we can never experience in this life all of who He is. At times, I have met people who came to Christ because the message was strictly about God being there to bless them, and it was hard for them to receive the teachings of Christ that called them to the deeper life in Christ. There was no hunger for more. They found it difficult to receive truths of the word that had not been presented to them before. The unfamiliarity of the word of God felt like a lie to them, and they rejected truth.

The temple progression of the Old Testament becomes a physical picture of a living progression as we grow in God. This does not require years in God. This requires faith that He wants us to live in the outer court of Christ and the inner court, and to dwell with Him in the holy of holies. This requires hunger to lay hold of all He desires for your life.

Again, we can look again at Jesus's words in John 6. These words provide a blueprint for His church to come deeper. He fed them by multiplying the loaves and fishes, and then He began to break open the truth that He *was* the bread of heaven who gives life to the word. He challenged them that they diligently studied the scriptures yet refused to come to Him. As we looked at in the last chapter, He then called them to become one with Him by eating and drinking of Him. It was at this point that many walked away.

When our hearts are longing to stay in the familiar because we feel safe there, God beckons us to move on so He can be more to us. We are called to live higher and wider and deeper than we have ever gone before.

Higher. Seated in Christ in heavenly places, seeing how He views things, knowing as He knows, and understanding as He understands. Ask Him to bring you up higher to see from His perspective.

Wider. We are having our hearts enlarged to receive His love for people all around us. He is stretching hearts out into deeper places of obedience to go.

Deeper. He is going deeper into our hearts so He can manifest more of His life and His love to us and in us.

> Then you will know which way to go, since you have never been this way before.

We are called to follow Him. Everything is about developing trust and a relationship with God. He doesn't want us to trust in the plan.

He doesn't want us to lean on our own understanding. We release an offering of worship to Him as we simply trust and obey. We oppose the standards of this world that rule with the mind, having to have every step laid out before they will take one step forward. Our obedience to move in simple faith opens up a path in the spiritual realm. Faith gets released, and mountains begin to move.

His word says we have never been this way before, as Christ leads His body into fullness of His promises. It will require a deeper dependency upon the Holy Spirit. We can't rest in how we operated or knew of God in the past. It won't work in this new season. Everything is unfamiliar. We are walking into the unknown, so we must keep pressing past obstacles that would hold us back from going forward. God has promised to go before us. He is the only one who can light this path. We must stay deeply joined to Him in this process. We won't be able to live on yesterday's word during this time.

We will be coming to Him continually to eat and drink of His word for life and strength.

Jesus, let the light from Your words illuminate the path for many to follow, which leads to fullness in Christ and eternal life—abundance, joy, peace, everlasting life.

Step into the River

> Tell the priests who carry the ark of the covenant; "When you reach the edge of the Jordan's waters, go and stand in the river." (Joshua 3:8)

There is a river that flows from the throne of God. Ezekiel had a vision concerning this river. In Ezekiel 47:1–5, he described it as,

> Water coming out from under the threshold of the temple. As the man went eastward with a measuring line in his hand, he measured off a thousand cubits and then led me through water that was ankle-deep. He measured off another thousand cubits and led me through water that was knee-deep. He measured off

another thousand and led me through water that was up to the waist. He measured off another thousand, but now it was a river that I could not cross.

The picture that is being painted in these verses is of the measurement of increase in the river and a deepening submersion of the man into the river, until the man was being carried by the river. This picture allows us to see the work of the Holy Spirit and the yielding to the Spirit in a believer's life.

There is a call of the Spirit for Christ's body to come into the river and to go out deeper and deeper. A new priesthood is arising who will follow Him into the river of God. This royal priesthood will stand in the place opened up. They will stand *in* Christ by the life and power of the Holy Spirit. There is a promise at the end of the chapter that I find exciting and compelling. As the priests stood in the river, a whole nation crossed over into the Promised Land.

The priests who carried the ark of the covenant of the Lord stood firm on dry ground in the middle of the Jordan, while all Israel passed by until the whole nation had completed the crossing on dry ground. (Joshua 3:17)

This new priesthood that is arising will stand firm on dry ground (Christ Jesus, our sure foundation) until a whole nation completes the crossing. What does this mean? All things become possible through Christ. It is said of David in the book of Acts that He fulfilled the purposes of God in His generation. These new covenant priests have had God's plans birthed in their hearts in the secret place. They see by the Spirit what He is doing and stand firmly in prayer, declaring Christ's authority, until the fullness of God's purposes are accomplished. This will require a strength of will and tenacity that can only be found joined to Christ. "Finally, be strong in the Lord and in his mighty power" (Ephesians 6:10).

As we look at the vision of the river of God in Ezekiel 47, we see there is life in the river, there is healing in the river, and there is harvest in every season.

We lose control in the river. It can feel terrifying. We become immersed in the river of God as we yield. Jesus said that out of our bellies will flow rivers of living water. The Holy Spirit comes to baptize or immerse us. If we don't fight it, but just yield, we will become fully immersed in the river. The river will carry us to where God wants us to go. We must move out and allow God to have more and more control.

In Alaska, there are beautiful rivers that provide a visual on this reality. People come from all over in the summertime to fish for salmon. When I sit by the river, my soul finds peace just watching the movement of the river. It reminds me of God's river. As we sit with Christ, we are drawn into the river of God, and there is peace that comes to us as are hearts are stilled and we yield to the Holy Spirit's moving upon our hearts. We hear God's heartbeat in this place. We begin to move with God.

Prayer: God, have Your way. We love You, Jesus. We love Your ways. Whatever, wherever, Lord!

7

Who Can Stand in His Glory?

"Who can stand in My glory?" This question that exploded in my spirit almost knocked me off my treadmill one day early into our adventure in Alaska. It left me not standing, but on my face before a holy God as I felt the weight of His glory pressing on my heart.

We are called to be changed by His glory. We are called to reflect His glory, but on that day, it left me wondering, "Who *can* stand in His glory?" The Lord began to speak to me about a consecrated priesthood.

The Purpose of Consecration

So I will consecrate the Tent of meeting and the altar and will consecrate Aaron and his sons to serve me as priests. Then I will dwell among the Israelites and be their God. They will know that I am the Lord their God, who brought them out of Egypt so that I might dwell among them. I am the Lord their God. (Exodus 29:44–45)

Again, God's heart that longs to dwell among us is revealed in these verses. Through Christ, we enter into restored fellowship with God.

Again, we see a progression in this restored fellowship. In the outer court, we find salvation and blessings in Christ through His perfect sacrifice, and we find blessing at the laver as we are washed with the water of the word. In the inner court, we find transformation in Christ, and in the Holy of holies, we find consecration. He brings consecration so He can dwell with us and among us. He desires this so much.

The Hebrew root definition for the word consecrate is *qadash,* which means "to be set apart." The *Webster's Dictionary* definition of the word *consecration* means to "be dedicated to a sacred purpose." What is His sacred purpose for you? He has a good plan and purpose for your life. Seasons of consecration bring about an ever-sharpening focus to seek first the kingdom and His will and ways in all things. The work of consecration brings us into a place of being God focused instead of self-focused in our lives and in our prayers. We become full of His love and His holiness, and our motives are purified. The work of consecration is where an ever-deepening surrender to Him happens, where everything that would exalt itself against the lordship of Jesus Christ in our lives bows to Him and all things in our lives are made new.

Several years ago, as I was studying consecration, the Lord asked me a question.

> Why do hearts stay in religious systems of "coming to church"? He was not looking for my answer but wanted to give me His answer. He then said to me, "In a system of coming to church, people try to have Me on their terms and the deepest desires of hearts don't have to be offered up and surrendered to Me."

First Corinthians 10:31 says, "Whether therefore you eat or drink or whatsoever you do, do all to the glory of God." Seasons of consecration bring about an ever-deepening focus of living for the glory of God in all things. The Old Testament picture in Exodus 29 is a one-time consecration that they might serve as priests. For new covenant priests, we go from glory to glory to become like Him. It is the sanctifying work of the Spirit in our lives. First Thessalonians 5:23 says, "May God himself, the God of peace, sanctify you through and through." It is God doing the work as we yield to this work to purify and join our whole spirit, soul, and body to Him that He might dwell with us.

God never strips away without adding back in fuller measure. Exodus 28 describes the garments the priests would be clothed in. They first had to be stripped down and washed. God wants us to view the sanctifying seasons of our lives differently. These seasons of consecration come to us not as punishment. His purpose in them are born out of His longing to be with us and for us to be with Him. It is for the purpose of us being clothed with heaven's realities.

In Exodus 28, there is the description of what the priests' garments would look like. Exodus 28:40 says, "Make tunics, sashes and headbands for Aaron's sons, to give them dignity and honor." The NKJV says to "give them glory and beauty."

The washing with the water of the word cleans our view of how we see God, ourselves and others. The washing with the water of the word changes how we live and what we live for. As we are clothed with the glory and beauty of our heavenly Father's kingdom, we won't have to strive to find dignity and honor from the car we drive or the house we own or the job and/or ministry position we hold. God wants to give us value and worth in the deepest places of our hearts. These seasons of consecration will clothe us with heaven's realities.

> You are all sons of God through faith in Christ Jesus, for all of you who were baptized into Christ have *clothed yourselves with Christ*. There is neither Jew nor Greek, slave nor free, male nor female, for you are all one in Christ Jesus. (Galatians 3:26–28)
>
> May your priests be *clothed* with righteousness; may your saints sing for joy. (Psalm 132:9)
>
> I am going to send you what my Father has promised; but stay in the city until you have been *clothed* with power from on high. (Luke 24:49)

> Surely you will summon nations you know not, and nations that do not know you will hasten to you, because of the Lord your God, the Holy One of Israel, for he has *clothed* you with splendor. (Isaiah 55:5–6)

As the culture of His kingdom comes to penetrate, it begins to challenge and overthrow every other reality. He desires that we understand and embrace His ways and processes. Seasons of consecration clothe our hearts with His truth in our innermost parts. The Lord told Jeremiah He was appointing Him over nations and kingdoms to "uproot, and tear down, to destroy and overthrow, to build and to plant" (Jeremiah 1:10). His kingdom ways are being worked deeply into our own hearts and His authority in prayer to release His kingdom, because we have been joined to Christ. God desires to uproot, tear down, and destroy everything that would attempt to exalt itself against the lordship of Jesus Christ in our lives.

We are continually being changed by Him. There are seasons of consecration as He goes deeper and deeper. There are seasons of consecration as lesser things fall away as God's holy purpose for your life grips more and more. There are seasons of consecration in new seasons to prepare us for new works. God spoke to Joshua of consecration in preparation of their crossing over. He was preparing them to walk differently in a new season. "Joshua told the people, 'Consecrate yourselves, for tomorrow the Lord will do amazing things among you'" (Joshua 3:5).

God was about to do something supernatural among them to bring them into a long-delayed promise. He was calling them to prepare in consecration.

The Process of Consecration

When we read through Exodus 29, we gain insight into God's ways concerning this preparation of a spiritual priesthood in consecration. In these verses, we see the natural picture of the spiritual reality for new covenant priests of the washing with the word, the anointing oil, which is Christ's anointing, and the blood applied, which is the blood of Christ. Then in verse 18, we see the Lord say, "Then burn the entire ram on the altar. It is a burnt offering to the Lord, a pleasing aroma, an offering made to the Lord by fire." For consecration to occur in our hearts, it will require fire on the sacrifice.

The Lord gave my friend Trudy an acronym that was His promise to her for the word *fire*: For I'll Restore Everything. God's fire renews and restores all things. Where natural fires destroy, God's fire strengthens, not destroying us but everything in us that operates independent of Him. In the fire, we become strengthened in Him. When we embrace the fire of consecration, we are embracing the one who is full of fire. Ezekiel's vision describes Jesus in this way:

> Above the expanse over their heads was what looked like a throne of sapphire, and high above on the throne was a figure like that of a man. I saw that from what appeared to be his waist up he looked like glowing metal, as if full of fire, and that from there down he looked like fire; and brilliant light surrounded him. Like the appearance of a rainbow in the clouds on a rainy day, so was the radiance around him." This was the appearance of the likeness of the glory of the Lord. When I saw it, I fell facedown. (Ezekiel 1:25)

Jesus is full of fire. John in Matthew 3:11 said that Jesus would come to baptize us with Holy Spirit and fire. *Jesus, we welcome Your baptism of fire and Holy Spirit!*

The All-Consuming Fire

The fire is what comes to disable those things in our lives that have any other foundation but Christ, meaning anything operating apart from Him and His life. The fire of His love will join our hearts to His heart. It will disable our works and cause us to be joined to His works. The book of Exodus describes that the glory of God as a consuming fire:

> To the Israelites, the glory of the Lord looked like a consuming fire on top of the mountain. Then Moses

entered the cloud as he went on up the mountain. And he stayed on the mountain forty days and forty nights. (Exodus 24:17)

Leviticus 9:23 says:

Moses and Aaron then went into the Tent of meeting. When they came out, they blessed the people; and the glory of the Lord appeared to all the people. Fire came out from the presence of the Lord and consumed the burnt offering and the fat portions on the altar. And when all the people saw it, they shouted for joy and fell facedown.

There is joy and brokenness released in the fire of His presence. There is a consuming of the sacrifice in the fire of His presence. The fire of God consumes those things operating in our lives that prevent His love from penetrating.

In 2 Chronicles 5, the priests carried the ark of the covenant to its place in the completed temple. Verse 11 states

All the priests who were there had consecrated themselves regardless of their divisions. ... As they worshipped God, the temple of the Lord was filled with a cloud, and the priests could not perform their service because of the cloud, for the glory of the Lord filled the temple of God. (2 Chronicles 5:11, 13–14)

As they worshiped God, the temple was filled with the glory of God and the priests could not perform *their* service, because of the weight of the glory of God. This was the old covenant glory. As we worship God, there is a greater glory He is releasing upon His people. This latter glory, the glory of the new covenant, empties us so it can fill us. The priests of old fell down. A royal priesthood is arising who encounter Him and are "weakened in their own strength, and are filled with His greater glory. "

Disable us, God, from being able to operate apart from Your living power and glory. We want to see You, Jesus, high and lifted up!

Empty us so You can fill us with Your glory. This is a work we cannot do for You.

Every time we come to Him, before the His fire of love, we are changed from glory to glory.

The Searchings of the Spirit

In the fire of His presence, His Spirit is there searching the deep things of our heart to uncover those places where we are not living in dependence upon Him that we might freely be given His life. He desires to fill us with His glory. He desires that we stand in His glory for the sake of His name being declared in the earth, for His glory.

A holy priesthood is boasting in their weaknesses so that Christ's power might rest upon them. It is being deeply rooted in the hearts of this priesthood that apart from Him, they can do nothing. They have no righteousness apart from Him, no power apart from Him.

> My grace is sufficient for you, for my power is made perfect in weakness. Therefore I will boast all the more gladly about my weaknesses, so that Christ's power may rest on me. That is why, for Christ's sake, I delight in weaknesses, in insults, in hardships, in persecutions, in difficulties. For when I am weak, then I am strong. (2 Corinthians 12:9–10)

The apostle Paul rejoiced in being emptied that he might be filled. There was no joy in his own accomplishments, but he had a heart even into his last days on this earth of pursuit of God. He writes to the saints in Philippi and gives us insight into the heart of a new covenant priest of desire for Jesus.

> But whatever was to my profit I now consider loss for the sake of Christ. What is more I consider everything a loss compared to the surpassing greatness of knowing Christ Jesus my Lord, for whose sake I have lost all things. (Philippians 3:7–10)

A royal priesthood is inviting the deep searchings of the Holy Spirt for the purpose of being joined deeply to Christ. Holy Spirit, search all things. Search our hearts, and reveal God's heart. We receive from You, Holy Spirit, what God is freely giving.

> The Spirit searches all things, even the deep things of God. For who among men knows the thoughts of a man except the man's spirit within him. In the same way, no one knows the thoughts of God except the Spirit of God... we have received the Spirit who is from God that we may understand what God has freely given us. (1 Corinthians 2:10)

If we will bring our lives to live before His gaze, it becomes a place of exposure.

All hiding goes, all pretense goes. He uproots those places where we are living independent of Him. His fire burns away all self-reliance, which is independence that is born out of the trials of life that cause us to say, "I can't depend on anyone else, including God." His fire burns away youthful rebellion that says, "I want it my way." His fire burns away an orphan spirit that prevents us from being able to bond to His loving care. His fire burns up anything that keeps us from surrendering our control so He can be in control.

The all-consuming fire of God and the searchings of His Spirit in the process of consecration to join us so He can dwell among us. God is calling us to invite a fresh fire for consecration in our lives.

In this process of consecration, there will be times of supernatural encounters. We don't want to delay what can be expedited through encounters with God in His manifest presence. Moses at the burning bush is an example of this. This encounter with God changed him. These encounters are given by God to serve His purpose over us as we pursue Him. He leads us into these encounters. Invite these encounters to come. There will also be times in the wilderness in this process of consecration. Moses had supernatural encounters with the presence of God, *and* he had forty years on the backside of the desert being stripped of his own fight so God could fill him with *His* fight.

The Bible shows clearly that the wilderness can be expedited through obedience to the word. The children of Israel didn't have to go forty years in the wilderness. The journey could have taken thirteen days if they would have believed God and gone right in.

It took this long because unbelief had to die off from among them. The purpose of the wilderness was to teach them deep dependency on God for their daily bread.

He has been with us during the wilderness of testing, where the enemy of our soul challenged this truth with his lies that God has forsaken us, but the Promised Land is a revealing of Christ and His promises in fullness.

Daniel was given a picture of the end times. We are likely living in the final hour of this age. He is given the promise of a people being prepared in the place of consecration. "Go your way, Daniel, because the words are closed up and sealed until the time of the end. Many will be purified, made spotless and refined" (Daniel 12:9).

Who can stand to minister in the release of this glory of the latter house? These are the ones who are being set apart and prepared in the secret place of His presence to be full of His holy fire and to stand in His glory.

The Promise of a Latter Glory

The book of Haggai is the story of rebuilding Israel's natural temple. After seventy years in captivity, the children of Israel returned to the land of promise to begin rebuilding what had been destroyed. Sixteen years after they returned, God raised up Haggai to call them to stay focused on this rebuilding program. In Haggai 2:6–9, Haggai prophesies of a later glory that will fill God's house:

> This is what the Lord Almighty says: In a little while I will once more shake the heavens and the earth, the sea and the dry land. I will shake all nations, and the desired of all nations will come, and I will fill this house with glory, says the Lord Almighty. The silver is mine and

the gold is mine, declares the Lord. The glory of this present house will be greater than the glory of the former house, says the Lord.

Even as the nation of Israel waits to rebuild their physical temple again in their capital city of Jerusalem, God is building a spiritual house in this hour of Jew and Gentile, from every tribe, tongue, and nation, that will love God's chosen people, the Jewish people.

He is calling His royal priesthood up to a higher place of seeing what He is about in this hour. The focus of getting people to fill churches is giving way to a higher priority, a focus on His people *becoming* the church, living stones built together so an end-time harvest can be brought into Christ.

This spiritual temple is not bricks and stones and mortar. This temple is made of people. First Peter 2:4 shares God's heart and plan for this building project:

> As you come to him, the living stone—rejected by men but chosen by God and precious to him- you also, like living stones, are being built into a spiritual house to be a holy priesthood, offering spiritual sacrifices acceptable to God through Jesus Christ.

God is building a spiritual house, and He is filling it with His glory. His living stones will stand in His glory to minister because they have come to *Him, the* living stone.

It does not matter what is going on around us—the mountains shaking, the nations at war—God is working, and He is building a glorious house that will stand in the day of trouble and declare His greatness and power and majesty.

A spiritual house is consecrated, the altar consecrated, and a royal priesthood consecrated. Living stones are filled with a greater glory. Christ's body alive in the earth is bringing a harvest into Christ.

Joined to Him and One Another

His living stones will be joined to Christ and to one another. These stones will be represented from every tribe, tongue, and language. In an hour when racial tensions are increasing in our nation, these verses give us hope that at the cross, these divides can be healed, and hearts can be joined at the cross of Jesus Christ, for the building of *His* house that will be filled with a greater glory. No one is shut out from this promise. Christ's rejection gives all full acceptance into His plan.

> For he himself is our peace, who has made the two one and has destroyed the barrier, the dividing wall of hostility, by abolishing in his flesh the law with its commandments and regulations. His purpose was to create in himself one new man out of the two, thus making peace, and in this one body to reconcile both of them to God through the cross, by which he put to death their hostility. He came and preached peace to you who were far away and peace to those who were near. For through him we both have access to the Father by one Spirit ... And in Him, you too are being built together to become dwelling in which God lives by his Spirit. (Ephesians 2:14-22)

A holy priesthood is joined to Christ and fit together as living stones, God dwelling among His people and displaying His glory through the latter house He is raising up.

This process is not always easy. There is the rub as we learn to stay joined even in difficulties and conflict. This is not referring to casual, Sunday morning only joining. This is deep *koinonia*, the fellowship of the believers, true community. Jesus, You are the only glue that will bind us together.

We call forth God's house, His glorious house of living stones. We call every stone into its place. May every stone be set in place, according to God's plan. May there be no hindrances to where each stone is set.

The glory of His latter house is revealed through this spiritual house of Jews and Gentiles, all tribes and nations and people groups, made one in Christ.

As I was looking through an old journal, I found a word the Lord had given me. He is calling a holy priesthood to rise up and work with Him in His building project:

> Build my church, build my church—a church that has no walls, a body of people full of holy fire, carriers of my living presence, consumed with one passion, one aim— to see my ways established in the earth.

8

The Priestly Blessing

P aul begins his writings to the church in Ephesus with the declaration of God's plan and purpose for us and the fullness that comes through Christ:

> Praise be to the God and Father of our Lord Jesus Christ, who has blessed us in the heavenly realms with every spiritual blessing in Christ. (Ephesians 1:3)

A royal priesthood is arising, seated with Christ in heaven's realm and receiving there every spiritual blessing in Christ *to be released to others.*

> For He chose us in him before the creation of the world to be holy and blameless in his sight. (Ephesians 1:4)

A royal priesthood is arising, chosen before the creation of the world to be holy and blameless in His sight.

> In love he predestined us to be adopted as his sons through Jesus Christ, in accordance with his pleasure and will-to the praise of his glorious grace, which he

has freely given us in the One he loves. In him, we have redemption through his blood, the forgiveness of sins. (Ephesians 1:5–7)

A royal priesthood is arising in love, adopted as sons of God through Jesus Christ. A royal priesthood is arising, redeemed by His blood and forgiven.

In accordance with the riches of God's grace that he lavished on us with all wisdom and understanding. (Ephesians 1:8)

A royal priesthood is arising, with the riches of God's grace lavished on them with all wisdom and understanding, *to be freely given away.*

The Heart of God's Plans and Purposes

And he made known to us the mystery of his will according to his good pleasure, which he purposed in Christ. (Ephesians 1:9)

A royal priesthood is arising, with the mystery of His will revealed upon their hearts. It is God's good pleasure to do this. He loves to reveal His will to us.

To be put into effect when the times will have reached their fulfillment-to bring all things in heaven and on earth together under one head, even Christ.

In Ephesians 1:3–10 God's eternal plan and purpose are revealed in these verses: "to bring *all* things in heaven and on earth together under Christ." Jesus is the Alpha and Omega. He is the starting point and the finishing point. All things can be summarized in Him. Fullness in Christ is the fullness of God's plans and His purposes.

A royal, Melchizedek priesthood, because they are having their own hearts joined to Christ's love and leadership and know the goodness of His leadership, are longing to see *all* things in heaven and earth brought together under Christ.

From this union with Christ, there is knowledge of the times and seasons: knowing what the Father is doing by revelation of the Spirit. There is authority given to open up the reality of the kingdom in prayer, by the leading of the Holy Spirit, until all things in heaven and earth are brought together in Christ. They labor with Christ in the secret place, not by might or power but by the Spirit. This laboring is pure joy because they are with Him in it.

A royal priesthood is arising who are Christ's agent in the earth to invoke His blessings and issue His decrees and declarations. These blessings and declarations are activating God's plan and purpose of bringing all things in heaven and on earth under Christ. This work is for all: in individual hearts, cities, nations, and people groups.

A royal priesthood is arising, joined to Christ's indestructible resurrection life. The keys to His kingdom are being given. The power of His life is opening doors no man can shut and shutting doors no man can open in the place of prayer. His resurrection life is being poured out into situations through this open place of prayer and declaration. His is the most powerful kingdom.

The ultimate fulfillment of this reality will occur in the millennial kingdom. We are racing toward the end of the age, where Jesus will return and establish His kingdom on earth. We read the book and know, from now to then, darkness will only be getting darker, and His glorious light will only be getting brighter. The shakings will continue until all things are restored to Christ.

> Salvation and glory and power belong to our God, for true and just are His judgements. (Revelation 19:2)

As we move towards the end of this present age, will hearts turn and seek Him, receiving Him in His judgments that are true and just and be purified in these judgments? Or will hearts reject Him in His loving judgments and find themselves moving quickly toward a time when His judgments will turn to wrath?

There is a royal priesthood arising who are receiving His true and just judgments in the secret place and come out clothed with a revelation of His goodness, even as the priests of old were equipped with a declaration of His goodness in the glory:

> When Solomon finished praying, fire came down from heaven and consumed the burnt offering and the sacrifices, and the glory of the Lord filled the temple. The priests could not enter the temple of the Lord because the glory of the Lord filled it. When all the Israelites saw the fire coming down and the glory of the Lord above the temple, they knelt on the pavement with their faces to the ground, and they worshipped and gave thanks to the Lord, saying, "He is good; his love endures forever." (2 Chronicles 7:1–3)

In the secret place, this royal priesthood is receiving a revelation of His goodness, so they are convinced themselves that in all things, "He is good and His love endures forever." As darkness is increasing, a royal priesthood is standing in Christ, being sustained by His love.

These will be the ones who will walk through the times unoffended, fully grounded in the reality that He is good even when they don't understand all that is happening, able to pray with complete boldness, "Your will be done on earth" because they have settled in their hearts that *His* will is good and that they can trust Him in all His ways because their hearts have been aligned to His ways. Though they don't always understand, they know His heart. His heart toward us is good, and His ways are always perfect. His love is ever enduring.

His love is the most powerful force in the universe. What depth of darkness can withstand the power of His enduring love? Who will stand in this truth and declare this truth and sow these seeds till the hardest heart is broken down to receive freely? This is why Paul prayed for a revelation of the heights, widths, and depths of Christ's love to the church of Ephesians.

God desires to unveil His love over hearts and to fill a generation to the whole measure of the fullness of Christ.

Invoke the Priestly Blessing

God gave the words the priests were to speak over the people.

> The Lord said to Moses, "Tell Aaron and his sons, 'This is how you are to bless the Israelites. Say to them: "The Lord bless you and keep you; the Lord make his face shine upon you and be gracious to you; the Lord turn his face toward you and give you peace."'" (Numbers 6:22–26)

We have been given the ministry of intercession. We are joined to Christ in this. It is a ministry that releases blessing on others. Romans 8:34 says, "Who is he that condemns? Christ Jesus, who died—more than that, who was raised to life is at the right hand of God and is also interceding for us."

The Hebrew meaning of the word for bless, *barak*, is to kneel, bless. According to the Ancient Hebrew Research Center, the extended meaning of bless is "to do or give something of value to another."

The *Webster's Dictionary* meaning is "to invoke divine favor on."

The word *invoke* means to "appeal to God as an authority for an action ... the one who can do something for the one we are seeking ... needing something."

A royal priesthood is arising, standing in Christ's authority here on earth, releasing a priestly blessing upon those who desperately need God, even if they don't know or realize it.

In the Old Testament, God told the priests to bless the people and pray that God would shine His face upon them.

Jesus told his disciples to, "Love your enemies and pray for those who persecute you, so that you may be sons of your Father in heaven" (Matthew 5:43).

There will be a day of condemning all sin, a day of God's wrath, and then His final judgment. At this time, God is longing for all to come to repentance and find Him in His love and mercy.

Jesus sits on His throne, not condemning the sinner but interceding for them. A royal priesthood is arising, loving their enemies, praying for those who persecute them, and invoking a priestly blessing.

God gave the words Himself for the priestly blessing. Something very real transacts in the spiritual realm as His words are released through His royal priesthood. There is a real release of His life and presence shining upon hearts. A royal, Melchizedek priesthood initiates the activity of the Holy Spirit that establishes Christ's rule of love as they pray. They are joint heirs with Christ who are ruling and reigning with Him in this present age, as we prepare to rule and reign with Him in His millennial kingdom.

Imagine a multitude of individuals: men, women, and children from every tribe, language, and people group, living in the secret place, hidden in Christ with God, a kingdom of priests. His blood was shed not only to save us from death but also to raise us up to this high and holy calling.

> To him who loves us and has freed us from our sins by his blood, and has made us to be a kingdom and priests to serve his God and Father—to him be glory and power for ever and ever! (Revelation 1:6)

Jesus, we read Your words and we see Your love for us. We see that You are the perfect Bridegroom and High Priest of our faith, doing everything needed to purchase a people. There is a royal priesthood, a holy nation set apart unto You. Your priests are alive in Your love, releasing Your love. Jesus, You have opened a door over every life. Awaken hearts to this high and holy calling. May we pass through and enter into the fullness of what you have opened up to us of Your Father's kingdom and His glory.

> And we have the word of the prophets made more certain, and you will do well to pay attention to it, as

to a light shining in a dark place, until the day dawns and the morning star rises in your hearts. Above all, you must understand that no prophecy of Scripture came about by the prophet's own interpretation. For prophecy never had its origin in the will of man, but men spoke from God as they were carried along by the Holy Spirit. (2 Peter 1:19–21)

Finishing Thoughts

As I shared in chapter six, my husband Dana and I moved out from Seward, Alaska several years ago after being stirred by the Lord and His words in Joshua 3:3-4. The Lord was faithful to His word to lead us as we went. The path He opened up for us led from Seward to Wasilla, Alaska and then to Eagle River, Alaska. Last June, in 2017, after eleven years in Alaska, the Lord spoke to our hearts that He was calling us out of Alaska into a new season and a new thing. The new season He was opening up would lead us back to Omaha, Nebraska in September, the place for me where God had begun a new thing in my own heart many years ago. Back in Omaha, I would finish writing this book.

Over the last few months, I have been going through the finishing process of completing a book, with the book being edited, the cover design done, and then the inside design and formatting completed. It is amazing in the formatting process, the transformation that happens to the typed pages. Last week, as I read through the proof file that Lorinda sent me after she had formatted and made some corrections, the Holy Spirit stirred my heart to add these finishing thoughts before the book was printed.

God has used this finishing process to turn my attention to His words in Hebrews 12:1-2:

> "Therefore, since we are surrounded by such a great cloud of witnesses, let us throw off everything that hinders and the sin that so easily entangles, and let us run the race marked out for us. Let us fix our eyes on Jesus, the author and perfecter of our faith, who for the joy set before him endured the cross, scorning its shame, and sat down at the right hand of the throne of God."

The NKJV version of these verses actually describe Jesus as the author and finisher of our faith.

Jesus is authoring faith in hearts and He is finishing faith in hearts in this hour. Jesus has been writing a story that began with Him being chosen before the creation of the world (I Peter 1:20). In this hour in history, may this generation find their place in His story. All are invited into this story He is writing. We have a great cloud of witnesses who have gone before us, their stories from Hebrews 11 encouraging us on. May our faith be made perfect in Christ, and may we see His finished work revealed to our generation. Let us consider Jesus, let us fix our eyes on Him. Through Him, the new day dawns, the morning star rises in hearts, and a royal priesthood arises.

CPSIA information can be obtained
at www.ICGtesting.com
Printed in the USA
FSHW022345260819
61423FS